BAME: Breaking Through Barriers

*A Comprehensive Response to the Critics of the
Commission on Race and Ethnic Disparities*

By Hasan Ali Imam

Absolute Author
Publishing House

BAME: Breaking Through Barriers
Copyright 2021 by Hasan Imam
All Rights Reserved

Publisher: Absolute Author Publishing
Editor: Dr. Melissa Caudle
Associate Editor: Kathy Rabb Kittok

Paperback ISBN: 978-1-64953-247-3
eBook ISBN: 978-1-64953-248-0

Dedicated to my late grandfather, Mohammad Abrar Hassan, who understood the value of good education and worked hard to become successful. He gave back to Bangladeshi society by freeing poor people from poverty.

"There is another class of coloured people who make a business of keeping the troubles, the wrongs, and the hardships of the Negro race before the public. Having learned that they are able to make a living out of their troubles, they have grown into the settled habit of advertising their wrongs – partly because they want sympathy and partly because it pays. Some of these people do not want the Negro to lose his grievances, because they do not want to lose their jobs."

Booker T. Washington

Table of Contents

Abstract

The report on *Race and Ethnic Disparities*, commissioned by British Prime Minister Boris Johnson (known as the CRED report), came out on March 31, 2021. It is 258 pages and makes 24 recommendations to close the gaps in various outcomes measures. What should have been a unifying factor beyond politics turned out to be an explosive or even an implosive debacle in the eyes of many critics. I have read the report. I have listened to an array of vociferous critics. Now, I pen this response.

This book delves into the arguments made by the critics of the report, and I examine some references they have cited. I proceed to show that there are surprisingly many areas of convergence between the CRED report and its critics despite a disagreement about the existence or importance of institutional racism today. I identify twelve such convergences of thought. I also pose 44 questions to these critics and highlight some of their contradictions. The primary aim of this response is to engage in constructive dialogue and debate with these vocal critics for the sake of our communities.

The Need for Civil Debate – From Critical Race Theory to Critical Thinking

I have sent an invitation to discuss and debate to the most prominent critics of the report, for example, Dr. Halima Begum, Sir Simon Woolley CBE, Patrick Vernon OBE, Prof. Kehinde Andrews, David Lammy MP, and Professor Priyamvada Gopal. I will also deal with other critics of the report, such as Dr. Muhammad Razai's letter to the *British Medical Journal* (BMJ) and the United Nations Human Rights – Office of the High Commissioner.

A very painful saga has been the lack of civil debate; instead, I have seen more ad hominem attacks against the report's authors than solid counterarguments. The divisiveness I have witnessed should never have taken place, and this vital issue of addressing disparities in the BAME communities should have risen above politics.

It is difficult to ascertain how much Critical Race Theory (CRT) drives the narrative of the Left side of racial discourse in the UK. CRT came about in the 1980s from a Harvard academic and is becoming embedded in the American discourse. CRT assumes that all establishments in America are institutionally racist, run by White supremacists and that 'race' is a social construct devised by White men to subjugate people of colour economically, politically, and socially. The only way BAME groups would succeed is if these White, racist institutions allowed them to succeed when it served the interests of these White masters. CRT hasn't landed on our shores yet. A British minister, Kemi Badenoch MP, stated that the Government was against CRT.

I had the great opportunity and privilege to be interviewed by a well-known African American academic in the US, Dr. Carol Swain, ex-professor at Vanderbilt University and Princeton. She came from a very challenging background witnessing domestic abuse, fractured family, and poverty. Still, she lifted herself to a position of success by gaining five graduate degrees (including from Ivy League universities), becoming a professor at well-known universities, and commentating on many American TV and news channels about the state of 'race' in America. She told me about the embedding of CRT in many institutions in America, which has shut down debate and divided communities. Commentators who find themselves on the Conservative side of the discourse are cancelled. Many Conservative academics are fearful of being too overt in their views just in case their careers end. Dr. Swain painted a very bleak scenario, which I didn't think could unfold in America. It was like something out of a futuristic dystopian society only seen in movies. Her nuanced insights also led me to re-evaluate a few of my beliefs after imbibing the mainstream media Kool-Aid.

Thank God for the United Kingdom. The media still entertains divergent political persuasions. *'Cancel culture,'* which is becoming prevalent in the US, hasn't landed here either. I am still learning about CRT and comparing its principles to the arguments made by the critics of the CRED report. I think there is some unity. The destabilizing force of Critical Race Theory should be replaced by the unifying forces of Critical Thinking and civil discourse, a feat which this book will attempt.

My Approach to Debate

I am not afraid to debate with those who hold divergent views to mine. I will listen to all sides of an argument and be prepared to change my outlook. It's an education. I have engaged with individuals on the Far Left of the political spectrum concerning racism and protest after George Floyd's death. I captured this in my book, *United States of Anger. Why Linda Sarsour's Rage and Far-Left Violence Cannot Move Mountains. Thoughts of a British Muslim Conservative*. When I stood for Parliament in 2005 as a Conservative candidate, I respected my Labour/Socialist adversary for his commitment to his constituents and his adherence to Socialist principles, many of which were scrapped under Tony Blair's 'New Labour.' We got along simply fine.

I have also responded to my fellow Conservative compatriots on the Right of the political spectrum across the pond. I recently responded to an American medical doctor and her organisation (America's Frontline Doctors) in the U.S. who believe there is a conspiracy around the COVID-19 vaccine programme. The article is entitled *Debunking Dr. Simone Gold and Other Anti-Vaxxers –*

By a Fellow Conservative Compatriot. Link **here**[1] (links provided in the book will work if you are reading as an e-book).

I look forward to responses from her and the AFLDS medics. A well-known doctor in the UK who is also a broadcaster, fed back on my article. They will remain anonymous because of the political nature of the vaccine programmes. They said, *"Well done you for an excellent - frankly extraordinary - piece. Keep up the great work!"*

I have also engaged with the Far-Right White Nationalists. As a result, I will be coming out with a book that responds to their arguments, mainly focusing on the philosophy of the White supremacist terrorist who killed 50 Muslims in New Zealand. The book also includes a dialogue I had with a very odd White nationalist. It will be entitled, *Why the Far Right Are Far Wrong. Thoughts of a British Muslim Conservative.* The arguments against White supremacists are locked and loaded and ready for deployment. White supremacists should be prepared for precision bombing.

I state the above not to impress the reader but to impress upon them an understanding of my approach to debate and dialogue. It will be an insight for the critics of the CRED report of how engaging in debate with myself is likely to

---

[1] For the paperback version the website is:
https://hasanaliimam.medium.com/debunking-dr-simone-gold-and-other-anti-vaxxers-by-a-fellow-conservative-compatriot-8f8d163b9547

unfold, which will be positive, constructive, and productive. With the spirit of civil discourse in mind, I expect this book to generate some form of a civil debate with critics of the CRED report to find some common ground on our journey from divergence to convergence.

All the eminent critics mentioned above would likely be too busy to engage in dialogue with me. Still, I expect some retort from Dr. Halima Begum because of our common Bangladeshi heritage, common religion of Islam, and the same university we studied at. I also expect a response from David Lammy MP, a formidable Labour politician, and LBC Radio presenter. I have spoken to him twice over the last two years on Radio, and we do have mutual respect despite our political divergence. David has been vocal in his criticism of the CRED report; hence a well-argued debate on both sides would be meaningful and beneficial for all.

On the day the report came out, I rang the British radio station, LBC. I was one of the few people who called in to give general support to the race report after having to skim read through 258 pages. The brief discussion with **Shelagh Fogarty** on LBC Radio, March 31, 2021, can be heard **here**[2] (4 mins).

I spoke as a Bangladeshi Muslim who grew up in the UK from the 1970s onward. I am proud that my community

---

[2] For the paperback version, the website is:
https://www.youtube.com/watch?app=desktop&v=KmgK5qZX5qQ
&feature=youtu.be

has come a long way over the last fifty years, from a place of poverty and racism to a higher place of achievement, prosperity, and contribution to British society. There is cause for celebration, although the work still needs to continue. The CRED report reflected some of this success. I saw my community in this report, as well as other thriving BAME communities.

A few days later, after I had read the full report, I called LBC Radio again. I spoke with the presenter, **Maajid Nawaz** (author of the book, *Radical*). I stated I could summarize the 258-page report in one word -- **Empowerment**. The discussion with Maajid can be heard here (5 mins).

The CRED report was clear that overt racism still exists and that Government policies should be developed to address this. But it also recognised the achievements of BAME communities and their abilities to succeed and progress by overcoming barriers. The major thrust of the critics' argument is that the report let down the BAME communities because it couldn't find evidence of institutional racism, thus contradicting the lived experiences of institutional racism by BAME groups. I have noticed that most of the critics play down BAME successes over the last fifty years, instead choose to focus on our apparent perpetual subjugation. Racial and ethnic disparities are one thing; however, I am witnessing another unfolding disparity. The **attitude disparity** between those who believe BAME communities do not have the capabilities to succeed because of the oppressive

White racist institutions and those who believe that they possess the power, the tools, and the capabilities to succeed despite obstacles such as racism. This is the crux of the problem. Building a bridge between these divergent thought patterns will be difficult, but I will try.

Critiquing the Critics of the Report

Dr. Halima Begum, CEO of the Runnymede Trust

Halima has been on various news outlets during the CRED report controversy. Like many other vocal critics, the rage-o-meter was working in full swing because the report did not conclude what she wanted it to conclude. That there is no evidence of institutional racism today. The Runnymede Trust issued a statement on the day the report came out, and she facilitated a Zoom discussion panel that evening to attack the report. More on this in the next section.

Regarding her response, the reader can avail themselves of my two contributions on LBC Radio (pages 6 and 7). Halima also stated occasionally that she (her organisation) is here to stay and is not going anywhere. This is great. However, **BAME achievements and successes are here to stay, too, and the upward trajectory toward empowerment is unstoppable**. I believe this is the crux of the CRED report.

Both Halima and I share the same Bangladeshi heritage and the same religion but are politically divergent. This divergence gives rise to the different interpretations of the state of race relations in the UK today. A good example is this. Bangladesh recently commemorated its fifty years of independence. What was the Eastern wing of Pakistan broke free from oppression in the war of independence in 1971 with the help of the Indian Army. Every year we commemorate the freedom fighters for the sacrifices they made to create a new Bangladesh. Sheikh Mujib was the father of the nation who later founded the Awami League party. His daughter, Sheikh Hasina, is the current Prime Minister of Bangladesh. The person who announced the independence of Bangladesh on behalf of Sheikh Mujib was Ziaur Rahman. He became the President of Bangladesh after the assassination of Sheikh Mujib and founded the Bangladesh National Party. He, too, was assassinated. His wife, Begum Khalida Zia, became Prime Minister in 1991 when Bangladesh transitioned to a parliamentary system. She is now the leader of the opposition. It was a real credit to Bangladesh that HRH Prince Charles sent a message of hope to Bangladesh, as did Prime Minister Boris Johnson. The Conservative MP, Paul Scully, was responsible for the lighting of the London Eye in green and red, representing the colours of the Bangladesh flag. A moment of pride for all British Bangladeshis.

Now that I have put Bangladesh on the map in this book, here is an interesting disparity between myself and Halima on how we interpret the progress of Bangladesh and its diaspora in the UK. On the day of the commemoration of independence, I rang LBC Radio (I am a regular caller). I spoke with Ian Dale, expressing pride in how far Bangladesh has come in the last fifty years, including the British Bangladeshi community. The link to the 2-min discussion can be heard here[3]. The country that Henry Kissinger once regarded as a bottomless basket, which was also seen as a flood-ridden and poverty-stricken country, is now a middle-income nation. It is one of the fastest-growing economies in Asia and on course to become a developed nation within a few decades. A few years ago, it accommodated 700,000 Rohingya refugees from Burma. A nation that was taking, it is now giving.

On a UK diaspora level, our community was perceived as being poor, from a developing country thirty years ago. Racism was real, exemplified by the murder of Quddus Ali in 1993 by White racists (the same year that Stephen Lawrence died). I remember this incident well. Thirty years later, I see prosperity in my community. There are British-Bangladeshi millionaires, which were unheard of thirty years ago. Educational attainment is improving, and we are now contributing to society. I was proud that fellow British Bangladeshis involved with the Conservative Party (Conservative Friends of Bangladesh) took a group of Conservative MPs to Bangladesh to visit the Rohingya

---

[3] For the paperback version, the website is:
https://www.youtube.com/watch?app=desktop&v=z9-TxMdyAL8&feature=youtu.be

Refugees. Because of this visit, the Department for International Development increased its aid by tens of millions of Pounds to help these refugees. A stunning achievement by a small group of British Bangladeshis. I cannot hide my pride in the three Labour MPs of Bangladeshi origin, despite our 180 degrees of divergence in our politics. There is a lot to be proud of, and I hope to see more successes within my community.

At the time of speaking with Ian Dale, I had not heard of Halima Begum. She only came onto my radar after the controversy surrounding the CRED report snowballed. Hence, I was not aware of her article on the Runnymede Trust's website about Bangladesh's fifty-year independence and its meaning. She gave a good outline of the history of resistance, especially after the Pakistan Army had inflicted torture and deaths on freedom fighters. She also described the plight of Bangladeshis in the UK during the era of racism in the 70s till today. It is this *'culture of resistance'* that inspires her fight against racism. Unfortunately, she only wrote one line to acknowledge the progress that our community had made. This is our difference in outlook. She sees it as the culture of resistance against current White supremacy and institutional racism that is holding us back. I see a culture of prosperity, empowerment, and freedom breaking through barriers and is not holding us back. We see things differently because of our divergent political outlook despite our shared culture and religion. This may also explain disparities in thinking when trying to understand the underlying theme of the CRED report and the underlying criticisms put forward by its critics.

Patrick Vernon OBE, Sir Simon Woolley CBE, and Michael Hamilton

This panel was part of the Runnymede Trust Zoom discussion facilitated by Halima Begum. They are eminent figures in race relations and have contributed a lot to the advancement of BAME communities. The summary of the unique contributions of the panelists can be boiled down to a few bullet points:

- There was a sense of anger and frustration with the report.
- We should ignore the CRED report as it denies the existence of institutional racism.
- The report is not for 'us' (BAME groups); it caters to the White working classes in Middle England.
- The report should be burned.
- The report belongs to another universe.
- The report claims that we are all victims of our misfortune.
- The report glorifies slavery.
- The report claims that if the police stop you, it's your fault; if you have mental health problems, it's your fault, and if there is maternal death, it's your fault.
- This rhetoric was used to justify slavery.

- The report is, in fact, hidden eugenics. If Dominic Cummings, the former Chief Adviser to Prime Minister Boris Johnson, was still at 10 Downing Street (the Prime Minister's office), these eugenics would have been more open.

- The authors (mostly BAME) of the report are equivalent to Holocaust deniers being asked to write something against anti-Semitism. That they don't care about anything other than themselves.

- Structural racism (according to Patrick Vernon) is linked to power, which is linked to privilege, which is based on 400 years of enslavement and colonisation.

- Structural racism (according to Halima Begum) is about a Black nurse who could not tell her White manager that she did not want to be exposed to COVID-19 on the front line but that her voice was not heard.

- Structural racism (according to Michael Hamilton) is when forces come together which deny people of colour power and opportunity within society and deny us the benefits we should be reaped from society.

- Structural racism (according to Simon Woolley) maintains an order of White Supremacy. Simon gave an example of the vaccination programme where 60 million vaccinations have been administered worldwide but in Africa where only 25 people had been vaccinated.

- The report is about divide and rule.

- When Halima asked the panel if there was anything positive about the report, the majority answered, 'no.' There was one positive aspect of family aspirations for their children.
- In the end, there was a call to action by Halima to mobilise against the Government and to find allies.

The most puzzling contributions came from Patrick Vernon, who said he wore a Star Trek uniform earlier in the day on a BBC news programme to prove that the CRED report belonged to another universe. As a Trekkie, myself minus the uniform (because my wife threw it away), I believe that the report belongs to our universe, in our timeline, or maybe the report is slightly ahead of its time. Why? Because it recognises successes that our BAME communities have made because we have the capabilities and ingenuity to do so (of course, the Government has a role in providing opportunities for us), the tools that the critics believe we don't have because of institutional racism. Patrick made a severe charge of eugenics in this report. He should have been called out for it but wasn't, although Halima stopped him because even she seemed surprised with his claim. I have seen nothing remotely related to eugenics in the 258-page report. When he also advocated for the burning of the report, the rage-o-meter was working fine to raise the anger levels of BAME communities.

The critics accusing the CRED report of blaming people for their poor outcomes is a peculiar insight given that it never indicated that. **Far from blaming people for poor**

outcomes, the report did the opposite; it credited people for good outcomes in some areas of education and economics despite barriers. The report is unique because it drills down to the root causes of the various adverse outcomes of many communities. It offers suggestions on how to overcome them through a series of recommendations, which include Government policy interventions, contrary to the narrative played out by the critics where they claim the Government would sit back and do nothing. They clearly haven't read the report.

Regarding COVID-19 vaccines in Africa, Simon said only twenty-five people had been vaccinated at the Zoom discussion. Thirteen million Africans had been vaccinated, and a vaccine producer had pledged to distribute 400 million vaccines as part of a deal with the African Union.

Simon stated that the report was not for 'us' because it referred to White working classes who seemed to have fallen behind BAME groups in some areas. Another criticism that the report should not have included data on more impoverished White communities because it was about BAME disparities. This insight is driven by division and discord and flies against the goal we all want to achieve: equity and an even playing field. If some BAME groups are doing better than some White groups, it is right to highlight this. It shows that some progress is being made. Some BAME groups are excelling compared to their White counterparts, which was inconceivable fifty years ago. Why should this not be reported? Because it goes against the critics' narrative that progress has not been made because of our perpetual subjugation from the White supremacist institutional racism.

At the end of the discussion, Halima wished that the report mentioned COVID-19 and BAME groups. It did, on page 220. When Halima gave the call to action to mobilise and find allies, a Socialist/Marxist thing to do (recall that Halima and myself attended the same university where the Socialist Workers group and the Revolutionary Communist Party were active on campus), we are all here. All of us are allies against racism despite political differences.

More on institutional racism later. I also have an issue with Sir Simon Woolley CBE (Lord Woolley of Woodford) and Patrick Vernon OBE, which I will also deal with later. The clue is in their titles.

Professor Kehinde Andrews, Birmingham City University

Kehinde is a professor of Black Studies at Birmingham City University. He is the first Black studies professor who instituted a Black studies programme in Europe. I first came across him in 2020 after George Floyd's death in an article he wrote for the British newspaper, The Guardian. He wasn't impressed with more BAME diversity within the Cabinet of Prime Minister Boris Johnson because they are Right-wing in their political views. He even criticised the formidable Secretary of State under President Bush's administration, Condoleezza Rice. Despite many of her qualities and contributions, the fault he found was that she went on a shopping spree during the Hurricane Katrina disaster, something she called herself out on in her biography. As I will show later, this is the racism of groupthink, that your skin colour must determine a specific political alignment.

In one of the Sky TV documentaries on Black Lives Matter, Kehinde stated that the economic system would need to be brought down to achieve racial justice. He was referring to Capitalism, which he equates with racism. He wrote a book entitled *The New Age of Empire. How Racism and Colonialism Still Rule the world.* The description of the book states, *"The West is rich because the Rest is poor. Capitalism is racism. The West congratulates itself on raising poverty by increments in the developing world while ignoring the fact that it created these conditions in the first place and continues to perpetuate them."* There is an obvious underlying anti-Capitalist narrative driving the post-Floyd protest movements. It is regrettable how groups exploited the death of George Floyd and his family's subsequent misery with a specific plan to bring down Capitalism/Conservatism. This economic and political ideology has raised millions of people out of poverty around the world. This is not an academic discourse; the practical evidence is there for all to see. Capitalism is the target now, and religion is on the periphery.

In his interview with Julia Hartley-Brewer on Talk Radio UK, Kehinde said he would grade the report a zero. He was again condemning it for its denial of institutional racism. The report stated that there was an interplay of different factors other than racism that generated poor outcomes in many BAME groups and even White working-class groups. They are geography, class, culture, family, economics, etc. Kehinde agreed on these issues, but with a caveat that these other factors are driven by institutional racism.

This is another crux of the problem in the debate. The CRED report explicitly states that racism is still overt but other factors mentioned above impact outcomes. The critics state that these have the point of origin in institutional racism. There is some overlap in the thinking on both sides. This is the convergence I mentioned in my introduction. They would both agree on these other factors of culture, class, geography, etc. but disagree on whether racism is the progenitor. There is an acid test on which side is correct:

A) If institutional racism is the key driver, then changing the other factors will not improve outcomes for the BAME groups.

B) If racism is not the key driver, then changing these other factors would improve the conditions of BAME groups.

What does the evidence show over the last fifty years? Are BAME groups in a better place today compared to their grandparents or not? Are BAME groups succeeding more so than fifty years ago or not? The answer should be obvious.

While Kehinde would mark the CRED report a zero, I will give my book here a cautious seven out of ten. Once I receive responses from the invitees and engage in civil debate, the mark should rise to eight plus out of ten.

David Lammy MP

David is a formidable veteran Labour MP in the UK. With Afro-Caribbean heritage, he has been at the forefront of leading the campaigns against racism. A few years ago, he was commissioned by the Government to undertake a review of the criminal justice system. He came out with the *Lammy Review*. The CRED report refers to this review.

In his passionate criticism of the CRED report on LBC Radio, David cited examples of Black families who had been at the brunt of racism. The fact that the report denied the existence of institutional racism deeply offended him.

I address institutional racism later. But one of question I would ask David is this:

Question 1: Is his success as a formidable parliamentarian and a radio presenter because of his strengths and volitions, which helped him overcome barriers or is it because of the White men in racist institutions that allowed him to succeed because it served their interests as Critical Race Theory would have it?

The report's optimism of BAME successes forms the foundation of the 258-page report. David made a similar comment in his review. The very first paragraph states, *"Across England and Wales, people from minority ethnic backgrounds are breaking through barriers. More students from Black, Asian, and Minority Ethnic (BAME) backgrounds are achieving in school and going to university. There is a growing BAME middle class. Powerful, high-profile institutions, like the House of Commons, are slowly becoming more diverse. Yet our justice system bucks the trend."* (*Lammy Review*, p. 3)

David on LBC Radio stated he wants to see the page turn on the racism issue. I believe the CRED report is that page-turner he is looking for despite his scathing attacks on it.

BBC Newsnight Debate with Calvin Robinson, Nadine Batchelor-Hunt, and Bell Ribeiro-Addy MP

A BBC Newsnight debate was held with various participants, facilitated by the BBC anchor, Katie Razzal.

One of the report authors was Dr. Samir Shah, and he was interviewed about the findings. He was clear that the report was evidence-based, and while it did not deny institutional racism, there was no evidence of it. But it confirmed the existence of overt racism. The debate then ensued with a panel consisting of the journalist, Calvin Robinson, who supported the report's findings, and two critics of the report. They were the Labour MP, Bell Ribeiro-Addy, and the journalist, Nadine Batchelor-Hunt -- a White-privileged name.

Calvin confirmed the existence of racism but that there was no evidence of institutional racism. The other factors of class, culture, geography, etc., are the overriding factors that determined success rather than race. The two critics, Nadine and Bell, were quite passionate in their riposte. Institutional racism came up again, and they argued it was the central theme that explains poor outcomes.

Nadine assumed that "***Black people would reject the report***." How does she know this? Black communities form around 3.4% of the UK population, approximately 2.3 million. Let's assume there are over 1 million Black adults (I am excluding teenagers for simplicity). For Nadine's claim to be correct, these one million people would need to have read the entire 258 pages and assess the evidence presented. Then a survey would have to be conducted to find out what proportion of Black adults disagreed with the report. All of this could not have been done within one day of the publication of the report. So, why did she assume that most Black people would reject it? What she is doing is imposing her assumption on one million individuals. She expects one million Black people to conform by disagreeing with the report because of their race. It is the bigotry/racism of conformity because of certain skin colour.

Nadine also claimed that the report blamed poor outcomes in BAME communities on themselves. The same claim was made during the Runnymede Trust panel discussion. The report does not lay blame on the BAME communities themselves if there are poor outcomes. But give credit to them for good outcomes, a credit that critics of the report refuse to give.

When Bell was asked whether there was anything positive in the twenty-four recommendations, she answered that some were, "...*well-intentioned but wishy-washy*." Reading between the lines, this means she agreed with some recommendations. So, which recommendations did she agree with and why? Objectivity demands that where she agrees with the report, she expresses this confidently without fear of retaliation from the powers within her Labour Party or Socialist activists. She added her comments, 'wishy- washy' to avoid Katie pursuing her on the recommendations she agreed with. I base the 24 recommendations on data and evidence; they cannot be deemed to be wishy-washy.

I know that other critics have questioned the data in the CRED report or have accused the authors of being selective. This is where my invitation to the critics for dialogue and debate is warranted. We can then delve into details of the data presented in the report and examine which dataset is selective or wrong and what the correct data should show.

Professor Priyamvada Gopal

I first came across Priyamvada when the CRED report was published (I don't get out much). She is a professor of post-colonial studies at Cambridge University and a fellow of Churchill College. I have viewed her Twitter messages, and she is active. She has been one of the most vociferous critics of the report. She did question whether the report's lead, Tony Sewell, had a doctorate or not. This is a fair question to ask because someone with good education credentials should oversee a report of this calibre. If Tony did not have a doctorate, then the credibility of the report could be questioned. So, if he had a doctorate, she shouldn't have a problem with the report's credibility. It turns out that Tony Sewell is Dr. Sewell. What an objective person would do in the light of such evidence is to admit a mistake and move on to examine and decipher the data presented in the report.

Cambridge professors can make mistakes, whether a small one like this or a large blunder that the late Stephen Hawking made when he thought everything that went into a black hole disappeared forever. The discovery of radiation emanating from black holes (later known as the Hawking radiation) triggered his paradigm shift. He grew some and admitted the biggest blunder of his career. Nevertheless, he moved on with his reputation firmly intact while occupying the very seat at Cambridge that Sir Isaac Newton held.

Enter another Cambridge professor, the late Sir Fred Hoyle. He came up with the 'Steady State' universe hypothesis, where the universe was in continual expansion because of matter being created continuously. This differs from the 'Big Bang' model, which explains the universe's expansion from fluctuations in the quantum field nearly 14 billion years ago. As evidence accumulated for the Big Bang model, Hoyle had to modify his Steady-State model. He may have been wrong here, but his work on stellar nucleosynthesis and the discovery of 'Carbon Resonance' led to him receiving a Nobel Prize. Reputation was intact.

Hawking's gargantuan blunder about black holes and Hoyle's humungous error in his understanding of the universe are far more riveting than Priyamvada's tiny mistake in the educational qualification of Tony Sewell. I know the reader will agree with me, with upward curves on either side of your mouth, known as a smile.

Instead of acknowledging her mistake, Priyamvada dismissed it by invoking the Nazi General, Goebbels, in that he had a doctorate as well, thus equating Dr. Sewell with Naziism.

Having traced back her contributions to discourses on race over the last few years, she has landed in trouble. After the Black Lives Matter protests, she tweeted, "*White Lives don't matter. As White lives*." She received a tremendous amount of racist abuse online because of this statement, which, when clarified and explained, does not mean what her critics interpreted. She invoked the equivalence of the caste system in India, where the Brahmin caste is at the top, and the Dalit caste is at the bottom. Side note: The caste system in India today is different from the caste system's actual meaning according to Vedic principles, where caste is not determined by birth. She means that Brahmin and White's lives are at the top of the food chain; hence 'White Lives Matter' should not be an issue because of the high status of White lives. In contrast, Black/BAME communities are at the bottom; hence their lives matter. I can't entirely agree with this interpretation, but leaving this aside, the racist abuse she received online should not have happened.

In February 2020, she chaired a debate at Cambridge, which questioned the status of Sir Winston Churchill in the light of racial consequences. She was criticised for this event. It is unclear whether Cambridge University had an issue with this event. However, she made a valid point where she called out the shutting down of debate by referring to cancel culture in the US where Conservative voices seemed to be shut down. She complained about why Conservatives continue to criticise cancel culture by the left only to shut her down because she has a different opinion concerning Churchill. Bravo. She now understands the challenges that many Conservatives (such as Dr. Carol Swain) face in the fast-forwarded future of American dystopia.

The Daily Mail seems to have attacked her a few times on various occasions, which could explain why she is feisty in her responses to critics via Twitter. The Cambridge establishment may view the eminent professor as a loose cannon, but that's ok. I, too, am a loose cannon, albeit tempered down.

There are three areas of convergence that I see.

First Convergence

The racist abuse she faced online after her Twitter remarks were horrendous. The CRED report referred to overt online racial abuse that has been on the increase. The report was resolutely defending people like Priyamvada, who has been the victim of overt racial abuse. She may have unashamedly linked Tony Sewell to a Nazi general, but Tony and the authors would still defend her from racist abusers. As Michelle Obama stated, *"When they go low, we go high."* Tony demonstrated this nicely by not bothering to sue Priyamvada for defamation which he has every right to do.

Second Convergence

Her lamentation about the pressure not to hold a debate about an issue she feels strongly about is understandable. We are talking the same language here. I do not know the CRED authors personally, but I know enough about them to state that they would not want to shut down a debate. On the contrary, they would advocate a free exchange of ideas without the fear of being cancelled.

Third Convergence

In Priyamvada's book, ***Insurgent Empire,*** the book's description on Google Books states, *"**Insurgent Empire shows how Britain's enslaved and colonial subjects were active agents in their own liberation. What is more, they shaped British ideas of freedom and emancipation back in the United Kingdom.**"* I have not read her book yet, but the review is music to my ears. When she credits enslaved people for their liberation rather than the White masters allowing them to, this flies in the face of the Critical Race Theory. CRT states that the White racist establishments permanently oppress minorities and allow them to succeed if it serves the establishments' interests.

What is more striking is that the CRED report's claims of BAME communities breaking through the glass ceiling through their volitions succeeding in many areas correlate nicely to Priyamvada's example of oppressed people having their power to free themselves. The parallel is striking. The parallel linescolour are converging.

Despite Priyamvada launching vocal attacks upon the CRED authors and the Chairman, Tony Sewell, there is an overlap of ideas unbeknown to both parties.

Afua Hirsch

Afua is a journalist and broadcaster. I mentioned her in my book, ***United States of Anger***. Like Kehinde Andrews, she

27

also dismissed BAME politicians who are Conservative. They have the wrong skin colour for the political philosophy they uphold.

She did not comment on the CRED report because she was fed up with the entire episode. That is why she requested journalists not to disturb her on the day of the report release. The reason for mentioning Afua is that her views on the British Empire and royalty are connected to a debate around institutional racism. She stated in *The Guardian* (April 15, 2021),

> *"The truth is that there is no escaping the haunting legacy of empire. Its ghosts have long taken possession of our royal family, turning them into emperors without colonies, bounty hoarders without raids, conquerors without wars. Instead, they are the heads of a Commonwealth in which the colonized are rebranded "friends" with "a shared history." This is fantasy stuff. Meanwhile, Britain's honors system continues to glorify the pain felt by survivors of colonialism and their descendants. This system, which two generations on from Prince Philip is still actively promoted, rewards British people for their achievements on remarkable terms. It asks us to aspire to see ourselves as "Members," "Officers," or even*

"Commanders" of the British Empire a painful act of betrayal to our histories."

Why is this important to the CRED Report debate? This is discussed in the sub-heading below, *The Empire Strikes Back with a Glass House* (p.63).

Professor David Olusoga

I consider David to be a more reasonable critic of the CRED report. He is a professor of Public History at the University of Manchester. He wrote an article in *The Guardian* on April 2nd. His main criticism lies in the report's apparent mischaracterisation of the history of slavery and poor grammar. He stated, *"As a historian, for me, the most disturbing passages are those in which the authors stumble, ill-prepared and overconfident, into the arena of history. The prose on those pages – littered with unwieldy phrases and bizarre constructions – is as weak as the arguments. In a sentence that reads like an auto-dictation error that got past the proofreaders and using a phrase that would get marked down in an undergraduate essay, the authors state that the "slave period" of Caribbean history was not only about profit and suffering."*

Like other critics, he, too, accuses the authors of selecting data and mischaracterising some aspects of education. He stated, *"Throughout the report, the authors rail against phenomena they either misrepresent or misunderstand. They defend the nation from charges no one is making; they create and then slay straw men and set up false binaries. Wilfully blind to the interplay between race and class, they are selective in both their sources and conclusions. The government has been quick to point to the ethnic diversity of the commission. What is lacking here is not ethnic diversity but diversity of opinion. "*

It would be helpful to understand what the straw men arguments are and what the false binaries are. The apparent blindness of the interplay between race and class is an interesting one. If race were the only factor that determined class, then there would be no White working-class families because their White privilege would have protected them from this downward trajectory in the social hierarchy. But I am open to a discussion concerning this. The CRED authors stated that race is no longer the explanatory factor for poor outcomes today and that other factors should be considered. This would have been a good debate to have, especially with David, but such opportunities were sabotaged by more vocal critics who have poured ad hominem attacks on the CRED authors.

One aspect I disagree with David is the end of his quote where he stated that there should be diversity of opinion. This is what was meant to happen. The CRED authors offered nuanced insights about institutional racism and BAME achievements, which are different from the conventional thought in the Left of politics that believes that by removing institutional racism, BAME groups would progress. The CRED report challenges convention; this is the remarkably diverse thinking that David is looking for. When such authors share insights that are divergent from the mainstream thinking of the critics, racist slurs are heaped upon them. These criticisms and ad hominem attacks are powered by the bigotry and racism of group think, that the colour of one's skin should determine his political and philosophical outlook.

Here, I believe, is an opportunity for convergence in thinking.

Fourth Convergence

David's call for diversity of opinion is a good one; hence, he must call out his fellow compatriots who have attacked the CRED authors (especially Tony Sewell) precisely because these authors have divergent thinking. It takes courage to do this.

Independent Experts of the Special Procedures of the United Nations Human Rights Council

The statement from the **Independent Experts of the Special Procedures of the United Nations Human Rights Council** (I will abbreviate it to SPUNHRC) was published on April 19, 2021, over two weeks after the CRED report was released. This panel of experts is a part of the **Working Group of experts on people of African descent,** Dominique Day (Chairman), Ahmed Reid,

Sabelo Gumedze, Michal Balcezark, and Ricardo A. Sunga III. I have captured some of the paragraphs of interest below:

...Among other things, the report blames single parents for poor outcomes, ignoring the racial disparities.

...The Report's conclusion that racism is either a product of the imagination of people of African descent or discrete, individualized incidents ignore the pervasive role that the social construction of race was designed to play in society, particularly in the normalizing atrocity. Again, the British state and institutions played a significant role.

...Stunningly, the report also claims that, while there might be overt acts of racism in the UK, there is no institutional racism. However, the report offers no evidence for this claim. Instead, it openly blames identity politics, disparages complex analyses of race and ethnicity using qualitative and quantitative research. It proffers shocking misstatements or misunderstandings about data collection and mixed methods research, cites "pessimism," "linguistic inflation," and "emotion" as bases to distrust data and narratives associated with racism and racial discrimination, and attempts to delegitimize data grounded in lived experience while also shifting the blame for the impacts of racism to the people most impacted by it.

...Instead, many racial disparities in the UK reflect specific nodes of power and decision-making by employers, teachers, and others who dictate the

opportunities and advantages available to people of African descent. Too often, this decision-making reflects legacy mindsets of racial hierarchy. In other words, institutional racism, structural invisibility, and longstanding inequalities have disproportionately impacted people of African descent living in the UK. Therefore, the suggestion that family structure, rather than institutionalized and structural discriminatory practices, are the central features of the Black experience is a tone-deaf attempt at rejecting the lived realities of people of African descent and other ethnic minorities in the UK.

...It renders inconsequential the fact that for over 400 years, laws classified enslaved people in the Caribbean and their descendants as non-human, chattel, property, and real estate, and social rhetoric and narrative evolved to rationalize, justify, and stabilize these injustices.

...In 2021, it is stunning to read a report on race and ethnicity that repackages racist tropes and stereotypes into fact, twisting data and misapplying statistics and studies into conclusory findings and ad hominem attacks on people of African descent.

...The Report cites dubious evidence to make claims that rationalize white supremacy by using the familiar arguments that have always justified racial hierarchy. This attempt to normalize white supremacy despite considerable research and evidence of institutional racism is an unfortunate sidestepping of the opportunity

to acknowledge the atrocities of the past and the contributions of all to move forward.

My thoughts on the above analysis are as follows:

- It is evident from the SPUNHRC statement that they had not consulted the Chairman of the CRED report, Tony Sewell, to seek clarification before launching stern responses. This debate should have been a debate and not division fueled by ad hominem attacks by the critics. Given the UN's role in peacekeeping, they just poured fuel on the divisiveness that the debate has turned into.

- The CRED Report does not blame single families for poor outcomes. A single-family unit is an explanation of poor outcomes. If this were to be applied to all races where single families were compared to the conventional two-parents structure, the single-unit families would have poorer outcomes in general (barring a few exceptions). This issue cuts across the racial spectrum. I would be looking forward to evidence that contradicts this. Let us revisit David Lammy's Review. There is another convergence of thought here.

Fifth Convergence

The Introduction-International Context section states, *"**Black children are more than twice as likely to grow up in a lone parent family.**"* This was a statement of fact and no one, not even the UN, accused David Lammy of blaming Black single-parent families for their situation. Neither did the UN condemn Barack Obama when he referred to the challenges of single-parent Black families. Before Obama became President, he delivered a speech at the Apostolic Church of God in 2008. About single-parent families, he said, *"You and I know how true this is in the African-American community. We know that more than half of all black children live in single-parent households, a number that has doubled — doubled — since we were children. We know the statistics — that children who grow up without a father are five times more likely to live in poverty and commit a crime, nine times more likely to drop out of schools, and 20 times more likely to end up in prison. They are more likely to have behavioral problems or run away from home or become teenage parents themselves. And the foundations of our community are weaker because of it."* (From Obama's Fatherhood speech, 2008).

The UN or the SPUNHRC did not condemn Barack Obama for blaming single-parent families. Like David Lammy MP, he stated one of the big challenges some families faced: absent fathers. When CRED authors made the same observations, the critics were quick to condemn them instead of working with them to solve this problem which is accepted by both sides of the debate.

In the Conclusion section of the CRED report (p.233), it NEVER states that racism is in the imagination of the people of African descent. Furthermore, neither the report nor its conclusion deny the past atrocities nor considers them inconsequential; instead, there is scope for optimism as BAME communities start progressing and breaking through barriers once thought of as unbreakable (and still thought of by the critics today).

Question 2: The claim that the CRED report data is twisted and misrepresented has not been proven. Which part of the data is suspect or misrepresented, and what should the correct data show?

Question 3: Which racist tropes and stereotypes have been repackaged into facts?

- I saved this one for last. The SPUNHRC response made a stark accusation that the report's commissioners tried to rationalise and normalise White supremacy. An in-depth reading of the 258-page report (234 pages of the main body, the rest are appendices) will not find any evidence supporting White supremacy. This charge is like the other criticisms levelled against them, of serving their White master prime Minister Boris Johnson or likening Tony Sewell to a chocolate bar that is brown on the outside and white on the inside. As Dr. Carol Swain pointed out, Tony would be described as an Oreo bar in the US. The SPUNHRC has ignored the overt racism, and conscious biases against the BAME-majority authors yet would seek to accuse them of supporting White supremacy.

I see it the other way round. **The CRED report poses a profoundly serious challenge to White supremacy.** White supremacists would like to think they are at the top, that BAME people are inferior and should not be allowed to succeed. As the BAME train starts to smash glass ceilings on its journey to the top of Mt. Privilege, the interests of White supremacists and White nationalists would be served if the narrative of perpetual White superiority and continual BAME inferiority is played out ad infinitum.

Although the critics generally focus on the negative outcomes of BAME communities, they would acknowledge BAME progress on different platforms when they are not discussing the CRED report. For example, we already saw David Lammy's first paragraph in his review that BAME communities have made significant progress by breaking barriers in many facets of life except for the criminal justice system. The optimism stated in Lammy's first paragraph was also stated in Dr. Halima Begum's last paragraph in her article for the Runnymede Trust, where Bangladeshis were progressing. BAME communities break down White supremacy and institutional racism doors, whose days are numbered and have nowhere to run. This is the crux of the CRED report, which its critics, especially the SPUNHRC, have missed entirely.

To the authors of the SPUNHRC statement, here are a couple of questions.

Question 4: What would your response be if your parent organisation, the United Nations, was classed as institutionally racist which needed to be brought down? I am sure you would say that this cannot be true as many BAME people make up the UN, and its top has been from

BAME backgrounds. You would cite the great work the UN is doing worldwide to alleviate poverty and instil human rights. I would agree with you. But professor Kehinde Andrews would not. Your compatriot on your side of the anti-CRED discourse has a more nuanced view. The description of his book, *The New Age of Empire* states, *"...Instead, genocide, slavery, and colonialism are the key foundation stones upon which the West was built, and we are still living under this system today: America is now at the helm, perpetuating global inequality through business, government, and institutions like the UN, the IMF, the World Bank, and the WTO."* Given what you stated in your response to the CRED report, you should agree with Kehinde. If not, why not? If you agree with him, that's great; you have exonerated yourself from the charge of hypocrisy.

Question 5: Why on earth are the eminent signatories of the statement (Dominique Day, Ahmed Reid, Sabelo Gumedze, Michal Balcerzak, and Ricardo A. Sunga III) affiliated to an institutionally racist and colonialist organisation?

Slavery is Not Celebrated. Neither is the Holocaust

A mistaken insight by critics of the report is the interpretation of Tony Sewell's statement in his forward concerning slavery. He stated, *"There is a new story about the Caribbean experience which speaks to the slave period not only being about profit and suffering but how culturally African people transformed themselves into a re-modeled African/Britain.*" (CRED Report, p. 8)

This statement has been warped into a celebration of slavery. Whatever permutations and combinations we can reconfigure the words to, they would not read, '*a celebration of slavery.*' Slavery was about profit for the White masters and the mass suffering of Black slaves. Afro-Caribbean communities have come a long way since that period. That is what the statement was referring to. But to up the ante and crank up the rage-o-meter to overdrive, Tony's statement was twisted on purpose multiple times. The report also made it clear that although there are stories of pride in British history, there are stories of shame (CRED Report p. 91).

An equivalent analogy I can draw on is the Jewish experience. Almost half of their global population was wiped out during Holocaust under Adolf Hitler. Six million Jews had been incinerated in gas chambers. It is a travesty and a dark stain on humanity. The Jewish communities came out of this and are some of the most thriving communities today, contributing to many spheres such as business, law, and politics. I have always considered the Jewish experience to be an inspiration to other BAME communities. They broke through institutional anti-Semitism. They said 'no' to White/Aryan supremacy and broke through barriers.

Now, I ask the reader to review the paragraph above. Do you see anything wrong with it? Do you believe that the paragraph celebrates the Holocaust? Or would you interpret it to mean that the Holocaust has been a cruel genocide (to eliminate the whole race) but that the Jewish community has come a long way without forgetting the atrocities? How in God's name did the critics of the CRED report lay the charge of celebrating slavery upon the authors?

Searching for the Structure of Institutional Racism

I have not made up my mind about the existence of institutional racism. I look at the evidence presented by both sides of the debate. I am open to sway, but I am formulating an opinion which I will share at the end of this section.

The main sticking point of the critics of the CRED report is its claim of finding no evidence of institutional racism. This is different from denying its existence. When the UN Human Rights group (SPUNHRC) criticised the CRED authors for not providing evidence for the lack of evidence of institutional racism, this is a circular argument. One cannot find evidence for a negative. Leaving aside the semantics, the crux of the argument from the critics is that the denial of institutional racism contradicts the lived experiences of institutional racism against BAME groups. The CRED report does not deny the existence of racism, even overt racism against BAME groups. '**The lived experiences of racism**' or '**lived experiences of institutional racism**' are the same statements in my view. What critics have done is to divorce the institution from human beings. An institution cannot exist as an independent automaton unless humans populate it. Human beings make the institution, not the other way round. So, when critics state that BAME people have experienced institutional racism, it is the equivalent of CRED authors stating that BAME people have experienced racism. They mean the same thing. Quibbling over semantics has damaged the state of debate on race in the UK when both sides converge against racism.

A major malfunction in the debate on 'lived experiences' is this. BAME and even some White folks would have had lived experiences of racism, but they would have also had lived experiences of successes. Why is this so hard to accept? Both sides of this (non)debate agree that there have been lived experiences of racism, but so far, I have only heard one side discuss and celebrate lived experiences of successes. These are successes that our forefathers fought for in the 1960s during the era of Martin Luther King Jr. and Malcolm X. They made sacrifices so that our generation may be in a better position than they were. To deny these successes and imply that nothing has changed over the last sixty years is a monumental insult to these civil rights activists.

Question 6: Was it worth sacrificing their lives if we are no better off than fifty or seventy years ago?

If you are a BAME reader of this book, we can both agree that we have had experiences of racism. We can also agree that we have broken through many barriers. Yes, or no? If no, please explain why. More work is to be done to ensure that gaps close, but please agree that BAME communities are on an upward trajectory, breaking through glass ceilings. If institutional racism exists, its doors are being forced open and White privilege is becoming a mirage.

However, it is worth delving into the arguments around institutional racism. I have more questions than answers. Consider the following sub-sections as me thinking aloud.

The British National Health Service (NHS)

The CRED report highlighted health disparities in many areas in BAME groups and White groups. However, it presented more complex data with multiple explanations of various health disparities rather than racism only.

The claim by critics that the NHS is institutionally racist is a bizarre one. I have dealt with employees from the NHS over the last sixteen years, and many of them are from the BAME communities and are reaching higher positions. The evidence of institutional racism put forward by critics of CRED is to cite an example where black mothers are four times more likely to die from childbirth than White mothers. Suppose a higher propensity to die of a complication is a sign of institutional racism. In that case, the same principle could be applied to White people who have a higher propensity to cancer. No one would claim institutional racism against White patients on this issue alone; other medical factors would be looked at. Yet, the same benefit of the doubt is not afforded to BAME patients who may fare worse in other health metrics. A simple test of whether racism drives the higher maternal death rates in Back women in the UK compares with Black majority countries in Africa. Are maternal death rates in Africa lower or higher (as a percentage of their population) than in the UK? If it is lower, then this may point toward some form of racism within the NHS. I have not looked into this, so I don't know the answer. But the CRED report does acknowledge higher maternity deaths among Black women (34 deaths out of 100,000) and that this needed to be better understood and explained (p. 228).

Let's take diabetes and stroke. This is something I do have an answer to. There is a higher prevalence of diabetes in South Asians. CRED critics would cite institutional racism as the explanatory factor. However, there is a high propensity toward diabetes even in Asian majority countries of India, Pakistan, and Bangladesh, where Asians run the institutions. Again, medical factors would be cited, yet for some reason, institutional racism would be the explanation in the UK.

Whatever the explanations for health disparities in the BAME groups, the CRED report recommended creating the Office of Health Disparities (recommendation 11) to address and close the gaps in BAME health outcomes. This is a good recommendation, not a bad one.

The reader would agree that an institution powered by White racism will not allow any BAME people to work in it, let alone rise through its ranks. Yet, we find tens of thousands of NHS employees from BAME backgrounds, and 40% of consultants are BAME. A White supremacy institution would not allow this. So, why is the NHS classed as institutionally racist?

One of the more credible critics of the CRED report came in a letter to the British Medical Journal (BMJ) by three BAME doctors. A part of the letter is quoted below:

"That structural racism is an important factor in ethnic disparities in health will not come as a surprise to anyone who has looked at the evidence. Several decades of research clearly shows that racism in all its forms—structural racism—is a fundamental cause of ethnic differences in socioeconomic status, adverse health outcomes, and ethnic inequities in health." (Mohammad Razai, Azeem Majeed, Aneez Esmail. Letters to BMJ, 31st March 2021)

In another part of the letter, Razai et al. referred to the Marmot Review (2010) to highlight that health inequalities have increased, and life expectancy was worse for BAME groups. I quote a paragraph from the Marmot Review below,

"...The two methods produced vastly different results, but both pointed to those with Pakistani and Bangladeshi ethnicity having the lowest life expectancy and non-British whites having the highest. However, both results could have been affected by the socioeconomic characteristics of the areas in which they lived (often known as the ecological fallacy), cultural differences in self-reporting of illness, and patterns of migration (for

example, recent migrants being healthier than longstanding and second-generation migrants)." (Marmot Review, p. 21)

Sixth Convergence

Interestingly, nowhere in the 172-page review do the phrases 'institutional racism' or 'structural racism' appear as the fundamental driving forces of health inequalities. The term 'racism' is used only once and in the context of socio-economic disparities, a view that aligns with the CRED report.

Razai et al. did pick out data from the Marmot Review, which showed the life expectancy of BAME groups to be worse than White groups. But when looking into other criteria in the review, there were some positives. For example, the quality-of-life scores for people over 65 compared the various ethnic groups from 2012 to 2017. The Pakistani and Bangladeshi groups had the lowest scores, but Black African and Mixed White/Black Africans scored on par with White British, sometimes even excelling (p. 24). Of course, any piece of data can be cherry-picked, so it is necessary to drill into the data.

Seventh Convergence

What is of further interest in the Marmot Review is the section on *Adverse Childhood Experiences* (p. 45). It gives a breakdown of nine factors that affect childhood adversely. Some of them include parental separation, verbal abuse, drug abuse, etc. And they looked at children from a range of deprivation (5 = most deprived, 1 = least deprived). The parental separation came at the top of the chart, adversely affecting children from all deprivation levels. Other critics criticised the CRED report for highlighting the problem of family breakdown, only to be highlighted as a significant factor in children's health inequalities in another review (Marmot) cited by Razai et al.

The letter also states, *"The report also concludes that deprivation, "family structures," and geography—not ethnicity, are key risk factors for health inequalities. However, it ignores the overwhelming evidence that systemic racism, in particular residential segregation, which is rising in the UK, is a major driver of ethnic differences in socioeconomic status."*

One of the references cited was *Brady D, and Burton L. in the Oxford Handbook Of The Social Science Of Poverty. Oxford University Press, 2016.* I don't have access to the handbook, but only snapshots of the abstracts of various topics that are available online. Working within this confinement, there is another interesting piece of data from one of the abstracts.

"...It then discusses the reasons why nonmarital families tend to be poorer than marital families and why the correlation between poverty and nonmarital family structures does not causally explain between- or within-country variation in poverty rates. It also describes some

methods for addressing high poverty rates among nonmarital household structures, arguing that policies other than marriage promotion would be far more effective at reducing poverty for nonmarital households..." ('Single and Cohabiting Parents and Poverty' by Christina M. Gibson-Davis, in the Oxford Handbook, mentioned above)

The above statement recommends policies other than marriage to address poverty in non-marital families, but it is clear that family breakdown and poverty are linked. And poverty would lead to worse health outcomes. They are interlinked. Again, Razai et al.'s reference to disprove the CRED report's claim of family structure breakdown being a factor in poor outcomes in fact supports CRED's claim.

Question 7: If critics still assert that there is institutional racism within the NHS, what would the NHS look like when it has shed its institutional racism?

Question 8: If you are a BAME doctor or in management within the NHS, what have you done to break down institutional racism (if you believe it exists)?

Geography

This is connected to the previous section, but I decided to give it a separate treatment. The same letter by Dr. Razai et al. focused on the systemic racism of *'residential segregation'* as a significant driver of ethnic differences in socioeconomic status in the UK. One of the references cited to support this is a paper entitled, ***Racism and***

Health: Evidence and Needed Research by Dr. Williams et al. (Annual Review of Public Health Feb. 2019). When delving into this reference, Williams discusses Racial Residential Segregation. He states, *"Racial residential segregation refers to the occupancy of different neighborhood environments by race that was developed in the U.S. to ensure that whites resided in separate communities from blacks. Segregation was created by federal policies as well as explicit governmental support of private policies such as discriminatory zoning, mortgage discrimination, red-lining, and restrictive covenants."*

This is an example of institutional racism that was part of the American legal and political framework in the 1940s. As will be discussed below, these laws were brought in by Democrats, who were the party of segregation, racism, and slavery. These form a part of their sordid history. However, the paper clarifies that such systemic racism of residential segregation was made illegal in 1968 under the Fair Housing Act. The effects of that historical institutional segregation would still be felt today. Dr. Razai has linked a past racist law in the US (which was later abolished) to increased segregation in the UK. They are two different things. The institutional racism of residential segregation in law in America was abolished in 1968. The effects may remain but are easier to deal with after the abolition of that institutionally racist law. The evidence from the US that Razai used to support his claim of increased structural racism of residential segregation in the UK actually contradicts his claim. The same paper by Dr. Williams states, *"In the 2010 Census, residential segregation was at its lowest level in 100 years, and the decline in segregation was observed in all of the nation's largest metropolitan areas."*

This is what one would expect after abolishing the residential segregation law, that such segregation would decline eventually. Razai missed this. However, more work needs to be done to ensure further decline.

Eighth Convergence

I have connected 'residential segregation' to 'geography.' The CRED report mentions geography, class, and socio-economic factors that override factors that determine poor outcomes in BAME groups rather than race. In the American example, the institutional racist laws have disappeared; hence, race is no longer the explanation for poor outcomes today. The historical remnants of institutional segregation have meandered their way through class, socio-economic factors, and geography. I believe that the CRED report and the letter's sceptical authors to the BMJ converge with geography and socio-economic factors. This is another missed opportunity to work together on this.

The importance of geography came into my radar when I campaigned in East London as part of my parliamentary candidate selection process for the 2010 General Election. This area had a high Bangladeshi population. What took me aback was the sheer number of fellow Bengalis who

49

lived in social (council) housing in a crowded area. What was also very new to me was the high frequency of police sirens I heard while on the campaign trail. I asked myself, ***how can my fellow Bengali brothers and sisters live like this in this part of London?*** A few weeks later, I took part in the candidates' hustings in the constituency of Bethnal Green and Bow, where I was up against two other candidates in the Conservative selection process. I made it clear to the audience that I wanted us to think innovatively, not how we could have access to more social housing, but what needed to be done to get more people out of social housing into private housing. Wealth creation is a crucial factor in empowering our communities and all communities. Unfortunately, I was not selected, so I don't know what I would have done to facilitate more wealth creation. However, a decade later, I see more prosperity in the Bangladeshi community, I see millionaires, and I see increased educational attainment. These tools will help BAME communities break free from the geography they have been embedded in because of historical segregation.

Education

The CRED report claimed that the education disparities between BAME children and White children were closing. However, some BAME children out-perform White children. If institutional racism exists, then we should not see this. ALL BAME children would be faring worse than their White counterparts in education outcomes.

Ninth Convergence

CRED authors were accused of divisiveness when they stated that Black Caribbean children performed worse than other Black African children. I heard this a few times across different debates, the charge of pitting one group against another by highlighting a difference in outcomes. However, in his Review, David Lammy MP stated, *"...In schools, for example, BAME achievement has risen but not in a uniform way. Chinese and Indian pupils outperform almost every other group, while Pakistani children are more likely to struggle. Black African children achieve better GCSE exam results, on average than Black Caribbean children. Wherever possible, this report seeks to draw out similar nuances in the justice system."* (p. 3). It is of great bewilderment why the same claim of education disparities between Black Caribbean children and Black African children has been attacked as divisiveness or divide and rule. CRED authors made the same claim and further recommended replicating successes to close the gap gaps.

Question 9: What would the education establishment look like if it shed its institutional racism?

Question 10: If you are a BAME educator within the system and believe there is institutional racism in education, what have you done to eradicate it?

The Criminal Justice System – Collective Amnesia of Black Victims of Homicide

David Lammy's review was primarily focused on the criminal justice system where BAME/Black men bear the brunt of stop and search by police and convictions. However, when Mrs. Theresa May became Prime Minister in 2016, she referred to the disproportionate amount of time Black men had to spend in the criminal justice system. This is the most substantial evidence that points toward institutional racism, at least in the penal system.

Both the *Lammy Review* and the CRED report (which also refers to the Lammy Review) acknowledge that Black men bear the brunt of the criminal justice system. Yet, surprisingly, some of their recommendations converge.

Tenth Convergence

The CRED report states, ***"The Commission believes that community leadership and role models are the heart of helping young people redirect their energies into actions that provide opportunities for progression in society and prevent their involvement in a crime."*** (p.159). The Lammy Review states, *"**Addressing high reoffending rates among some BAME groups, can only be done through greater partnership with communities themselves**."* (p. 6)

Divisive politics have sabotaged the opportunities for convergent discourse in the shared quest to improve the lives of BAME groups sprinkled with virtue signalling by the critics as they pumped coins into the rage-o-meter. The disagreement over 'institutional racism' is the sticking factor that overrides commonality and opportunities to work together. It has come to this.

While the *Lammy Review* looked at redressing the balance of representation between BAME and White criminals in the justice system, the CRED report has gone further to challenge policymakers to think of ways where BAME youths can avoid entry into the criminal justice system in the first place. It is well and good to equalise treatment of BAME and White criminals, a view which assumes that the destiny of many BAME youths in the criminal justice system. This is the bigotry of low or no expectations. **Let us stop youths from entering the system in the first place. Prevention is better than cure.** The CRED report suggests a reclassification of drug-related crimes, which would reduce entry into the system; moreover, it drills down to the root causes of youths getting into crimes. The remedies include police representation from BAME backgrounds in areas with a BAME majority population. The cultural alignment between the police force and BAME communities is a step in the right direction. Family breakdown is another explanatory factor that should be taken seriously, and again, finding out the root causes of such breakdowns has an adverse effect on many children and youths.

The most sinister aspect of the debate around poor outcomes in BAME communities is the complete oversight that Black men are twenty-four times more likely to be victims of homicide than their White counterparts. The critics of the CRED report rightly refer to statistics around increased stop and search among BAME communities or the fact that more Black women are four times more likely to die during childbirth than White women. Yet, they have all thus far avoided addressing this big elephant in the room. The figures for Black victims of homicide are significant, yet none of the critics have bothered to get angry or even delve into the root of the problem.

Question 11: What is the cause of higher homicide rates among Black victims? Is it institutional racism or something else?

These Black men are the forgotten victims of homicide, and the virtue signallers see no virtue in signalling this fact.

A similar mindset has been seen in the USA, where a teenage Black girl was killed by police in Columbus just before the Derek Chauvin verdict was announced. There was a wide condemnation of the killing of Ma'Khia Bryant. The timing of this so close to the Chauvin verdict that this could have gone nuclear. It almost did. I heard news interviews where the killing was fiercely condemned as another example of police brutality against a Black person. Yet, no one bothered to ask about the victim,

Ma'Khia Bryant, a Black girl who was about to be stabbed by the perpetrator, who in turn shouted, *"I'm gonna stab the f*** out of you, bitch"* as she lunged forward with the knife. While the police officer will be tried in court, and I think there will be protests to support Ma'Khia, no one will remember the Black girl who was about to be a victim of homicide. The policeman saved her life. Let's take the shooting of Jacob Blake by the police took place in Kenosha, Wisconsin, in August 2020. This was seen as another example of police brutality against a Black victim. While there may be protests to support Jacob Blake, the female victim of his sexual assault and domestic abuse (for which he had an arrest warrant) was forgotten.

Has the reader heard of Jaslyn Adams? She was a seven-year-old Black girl who was shot dead in late April 2021 in Chicago along with her father. They were victims of a shooting that was targeted at them by criminals.

Question 12: It seems from the above examples in the US and the CRED report's highlighting of Black victims of crime that these victims of homicide or violence are the most forgotten group of people. Why?

Back to the CRED report and the *Lammy Review*. Both seem to converge on the point of BAME youths involved in drug-related crimes. The *Lammy Review* also states, *"There is a settled narrative about young BAME people associating in gangs, but far too little attention is paid to the criminals who provide them with weapons and use them to sell drugs."* (p. 6)

Eleventh Convergence

The Lammy Review and the CRED report seem to converge on criminals themselves, especially in the higher echelons of adult criminal gangs. Lammy is looking at stricter actions on adult criminals in gangs, and the CRED report is looking at the root causes of youths joining such gangs. These two approaches are parallel but symbiotic. Lammy recognises victims' rights, and the CRED report delves further to ask how victimisation can be prevented in the first place.

I see areas of convergence here and an excellent foundation to discuss and debate to solve problems for BAME communities. But, alas, what could have been a fruitful discourse between different parties with similar opinions, turned out to be divisiveness powered by a narrative that states that the CRED report has absolutely nothing to do with BAME communities. I am hoping that this book would be the bridge to find some commonalities.

The British Parliament

If institutional racism exists, then it stands to reason that the Parliament, an institution dating back hundreds of years, is also institutionally racist. David Lammy did acknowledge at the outset of his review that Parliament is becoming more diversified. I agree with this. But using the logic of the critics of CRED, it is still institutionally racist. This means that the vocal critics of the report who are parliamentarians must be affiliated with a White supremacist, racist institution. Yes, it does mean that. The following Labour MPs have heavily criticised the CRED report:

- Sir Kier Starmer (Leader of the Labour Party and Her Majesty's Opposition)
- David Lammy
- Diane Abbott
- Clive Lewis
- Bell Riberio-Addy
- Dawn Butler

They would reject the assertions made by CRED authors and myself that systemic and institutional racism may have been the remnants of the past, and their effects could be felt today. Still, the structures today are quite different from yesterday. The fact that BAME groups are succeeding by breaking through glass ceilings is a testament to that fact. But the critics have claimed that institutional racism and the spirit of British colonialism are still in full force today and haven't changed. Given that Parliament has been one of the fuels that drove British colonialism in the past, it follows that it is still a powerful force of propping up institutional racism and colonialism today.

Question 13: What would Parliament look like if it shed its institutional racism? Why are the MPs mentioned above still affiliated with a White supremacy organisation steeped in colonial history?

The British Labour Party

The MPs mentioned above belong to the Labour Party. Recently, there were controversies around anti-Semitism which were seen to be deeply embedded within the Labour Party under the previous leadership of Jeremy Corbyn (yes, I am aware of the charge of Islamophobia in the Conservative Party, before the critics' pivot to this in their defence).

Question 14: Given that the Labour Party is an institution, then doesn't it follow that it is institutionally racist by default, in this case, against the Jewish community? If not, why not?

Question 15: Why are the BAME Labour MPs affiliated with a racist/White supremacist/anti-Semitic institution? What have they done to change it?

The U.S. Democrat Party

The younger generation may not know the history of the Democrats in the US. If they look at their website, it states that it has a two-hundred-year history of fighting for civil rights. This may be true in the last sixty years, but not in the previous one hundred forty years. Then, it was the party of slavery, lynching, segregation, and White supremacy, institutional racism at its finest. It was the Republicans under President Abraham Lincoln that abolished slavery to the fierce resistance of Democrats.

Why is this relevant to the CRED report? During the Democrat Primaries in 2019, Kamala Harris called out Joe Biden for his support of two senators in the 1970s who were segregationists and who opposed bussing. Bussing is where Black children were bussed to White-majority schools to help with integration. Segregation was a remnant of the racist past where anti-Black racism was an institution under the Jim Crow Laws. Democrats today would state that they have shed their racist past and have recently entered the civil rights discourse, once held by Republicans only. However, by extrapolating the thought process of the critics of the CRED report (who state that the institutional racism of past British colonialism and White supremacy are still in full force today) to the Democrats of today; it follows they must view the Democrats especially under President Biden, as the same institution of racism and White supremacy.

Question 16: Do the vocal critics of CRED consider today's Democrat Party the same racist institution of the past when it was institutionally racist? If not, why not?

Question 17: If the answer is things have changed for the better for the Democrats, as evidenced by electing President Barak Obama in 2008 and Vice-President Kamala Harris in 2020, why aren't they applying the same standards to the British discourse on race relations?

Lived Experiences of BAME Successes and the Failure of White Privilege

At the beginning of this section, I touched on the need to emphasise lived experiences of successes while recognising lived experiences of racism. There are numerous examples of successes. One such example has stuck with me. The Ghanaian-born Conservative minister, Kwasi Kwarteng, is someone I look up to. I used to live in his constituency over a decade ago. The way he got selected was interesting. At the time, for the 2010 General Election, the Conservative Party devised a novel way of selecting the local Conservative candidate. Instead of the selection being only conducted by the local Conservative group, the *'open primaries'* system was used in some constituencies. This is where a resident of the constituency could vote for their Conservative candidate regardless of which political party they belonged to; complete transparency. The various candidates took part in hustings in front of the residents of that constituency of Staines (which Ali G made famous). A local White female candidate was expected to win because she was well known and respected. I think there were about six candidates in total. After elimination rounds, the last candidate standing would be selected to run as the Conservative Parliamentary candidate.

When Kwasi Kwarteng spoke, I could see that he was way out of the league of the other candidates. His statesmanship, humour, and eruditeness shone through.

The audience was made up of around 200 people. I estimated that 98% were White. So, here you had six candidates, all of them were White bar one, Kwasi Kwarteng. The audience was 98% White. The favorite candidate expected to win was a well-known and well-respected White woman. The advocates of Critical Race Theory and the critics of the CRED report would see this scenario as the forces of White supremacy, White privilege, and institutional racism aligning into an ultimate orgasm of Black subjugation. Alas, this wasn't so. Kwasi Kwarteng won fair and square and is now a formidable minister (Business Secretary).

Question 18: How did this lived experience of BAME success happen despite White privilege and institutional racism? Why did White privilege fail?

I was pleased when Kwasi won; it was by pure merit. But, unfortunately, what worked in Staines did not work out for me when I took part in hustings in the open primaries in an East London constituency of 'Bethnal Green & Bow.'

Institutional Racism – The Search Goes On

I titled this section *Searching for the Structure of Institutional Racism.* I thought aloud about the topics discussed above, and I have yet to determine whether institutional racism exists or not. I have more questions than answers. But I do hold an opinion which is 'middle of the road.' All sides of the debate can agree on one thing. That there is an inverse correlation between institutional racism and BAME empowerment. If institutional racism is rock solid, then BAME achievements will not come to fruition. As we have seen above, BAME communities are breaking through and succeeding in many spheres of life. This leads to one conclusion only, and there is no room for manoeuvre. <u>If the structure of institutional racism exists, then it is crumbling before our very eyes.</u> Institutional racism and White supremacy are on a downward trajectory toward oblivion as they cross the paths of BAME communities ascending toward the stratosphere of empowerment, prosperity, and success. What is institutional is the collective, systemic thinking of incessant White supremacy and perpetual BAME underachievement.

If Institutional Racism Still Exists, then Have Race Equality Charities Failed?

The most vocal critics of CRED are Directors or CEOs of charities tasked to improve BAME communities' lives.

Question 19: If they assert that BAME communities do not have the power or tools to break through barriers because of institutional racism, which needs to be brought down to free BAME communities, how exactly have these charities empowered BAME communities?

Question 20: Tens of millions of pounds would have been poured into these charities over the last few decades to help improve the lives of BAME communities. But if they state that nothing has changed because of perpetual institutional racism, then these charities have failed, and the funds have been wasted. So, where has the money gone? These are the tough questions that need to be asked to hold these charities accountable for failing to improve the lives of their recipients because of institutional racism.

Question 21: If the answer is that things have changed, that their funds have helped hundreds of thousands of people, then why state that nothing has changed because of institutional racism?

Question 22: If they agree positive changes are happening and will continue, then why disagree with the CRED report, which us stating precisely that?

The Empire Strikes Back with a Glass House

We see the British Empire as a separate entity that colonised our forefathers from Asia and Africa. British BAME readers of this book will note that the Empire is not a separate entity; it is now a part of our history. We are the descendants of the colonised through genetics, but we are also descendants of the colonisers through our British nationality. The histories of the British Empire and the Royal Family are our common history now, not just a history of the English. We must deal with it. The CRED report stated that there are shameful parts of this history, such as slavery and oppression of subjects in the colonies. There are also positive examples of the history of our British Empire once it extricated itself from the curse of slavery.

This section is not a history lesson on Empire, but I want to draw the readers' attention to the honors system, which is inextricably linked to the British Empire. People who have made valuable contributions to Britain through charitable work or the arts or science receive certain types of honors from Her Majesty, The Queen. There are various grades within the honors system based on the impact of the outstanding work that the recipients have done. For the benefit of the non-British readers, the ranks are as follows (in descending order of importance):

- **GBE, KBE, or DBE (Knight or Dame)** - *Knight or Dame of the Most Excellent Order of the British Empire. A man who has been knighted would be addressed as 'Sir.'*
- **CBE** - *Commander of the Most Excellent Order of the British Empire*
- **OBE** - *Officer of the Most Excellent Order of the British Empire*
- **MBE** - *Member of the Most Excellent Order of the British Empire*

Many people have received these honors for their contributions to British society. An honor from Her Majesty would be a significant milestone in a recipient's life. I don't have a problem with the honors system because I don't connect it to the old British Empire of slavery and exploitation of colonies. It has a different meaning today, despite retaining the residual title of the vintage 'Empire.' The royal family today represents the Commonwealth of nations that had once been part of the

Empire but no longer connected to its negative past. Some commentators have a problem with the honors system because of what the negative aspect of the British Empire represented in the past. Because this negativity pervades their discourse today, they disagree with the system. That is why some people have refused the invitations to receive such honors from the Queen. A prominent case was the Black British poet Benjamin Zephaniah, who refused the honors in 2003. I respect him for his honesty. His principles are intact.

In a previous section, I mentioned the journalist and broadcaster Afua Hirsch. She criticised the honors system when she wrote an article in *The Guardian* about the late Prince Philip and the institution of the Royal Family. I stated I would revisit her here. Afua's rejection of the honors system is related to the past colonialism or the Empire. And given that the Royal Family and Empire are seen as institutionally racist today, it is understandable why she likens BAME recipients of the honors to traitors. It is difficult to read between the lines; hence, I cannot conclude whether she was taking a sideswipe at some of the prominent anti-racist campaigners who have received the honors. Only she can answer this. Here are the vocal critics of the CRED report who had cranked up the rage-o-meter when condemning the report, fuelled by virtue signalling. This is not a sideswipe; this is from the front:

- Sir Simon Woolley CBE
- Patrick Vernon OBE

Recall, they vehemently condemned the CRED report for failing to acknowledge institutional racism, that it wasn't for us. Recall that my fellow Trekkie, Patrick Vernon, wore his Star Trek uniform to prove that the report, which contains hidden eugenics, belongs to another universe. He also referred to a quote from the movie *The Rise of Skywalker*, when one character said, "*There are more of us.*" And he stated that the report should be burned. I am picking on Patrick Vernon because he made some of the most incendiary comments about the report, and he is a fellow Trekkie. Even in a Star Trek universe, we would see things differently. More on that later.

Sir Simon is a Commander of the '**Most Excellent Order of the British Empire**,' he has also been knighted. Patrick is an Officer of the '**Most Excellent Order of the British Empire**.' Taking their logic to their conclusions, they are affiliated with White Supremacy and a racist institution. Forget about the evil empire on the Dark Side in *Star Wars*; the British Empire is striking back here. It is a massive glasshouse that Simon and Patrick are throwing stones at. Cognitive dissonance at its finest.

David Olusoga OBE is an Officer of the '**Most Excellent Order of the British Empire**.' I mentioned him in an earlier section, and he has been vocal against the CRED report for its apparent mischaracterisation of the history of slavery. History is David's forte, yet he accepted an honorary title, the very title that he would link to White supremacy colonialism and slavery.

At this point, let me bring in the American playwright and commentator, Bonnie Greer OBE. I first came across her in 2009 when she was a panellist on BBC Question Time. That episode was controversial because the panel also included the Far Right British National Party (BNP) leader, Nick Griffin. I was part of the audience, and I did pose a question to him concerning his party's racist and anti-Muslim views. But to my disappointment, he was interrupted by Bonnie Greer before he could answer. Bonnie Greer subsequently received an OBE from HRH Prince Charles in 2010 for her work in the arts. Her understanding of such an award is more congruent with how I see it than Afua Hirsch or Benjamin Zephaniah. Bonnie described the award by stating that it was a *"Testament to the British spirit of generosity, of acceptance of foreigners, something I hope we never lose here."* The Empire and the monarchy no longer have the connotations today as they once did. The monarchy cannot be viewed as institutionally racist. The monarchy is the mother of all other institutions in the UK. If there is institutional racism, it will start with the monarchy. Given the new meaning that Bonnie has given to the OBE award and the monarchy, institutional racism no longer exists; otherwise, she would not have accepted the award. Yet, she would seek to discredit the CRED report by stating it was *"lightweight and a disgrace."*

These are not ad hominem attacks on Simon nor Patrick nor David, nor Bonnie. This highlights a significant discrepancy between thought and action, as they throw stones at this enormous glasshouse. Apart from the honors system, other titles recognize significant contributions.

Other than the House of Commons, where the Parliament and prime minister members sit, there is an upper house known as the House of Lords. The monarchy does not elect but appoints the peers who are members on the prime minister's advice, or they may be hereditary peers. The selected peers would have contributed majorly to society. Their remit is to scrutinise Government legislation. Their titles would be '*Lord*' for men and '*Baroness*' for women.

In the British legal profession, another title is bestowed on a barrister or a solicitor, who are high within these professions. The title is 'QC' (Queen's Counsel). The QC (or KC if the monarch is King) system was created in England hundreds of years ago and appointed to be one of 'Her Majesty's Counsel learned in the law.' The first Queen's Counsel was Sir Francis Bacon in 1597.

So, we have the honors system, peerage at the House of Lords, and 'Queens Counsel' in the legal profession's upper echelons. The vocal critics of the CRED report who advocate the existence of ongoing institutional racism and White supremacy would no doubt consider these titles to be firmly integrated with the institution of racism, White supremacy, and colonialism.

I laid out the above title system for the benefit of the on-British readers. Now, here is the relevance to the debate about the CRED report. The Runnymede Trust, of which Halima Begum is its CEO, has been very vocal in its criticism of the report (I mentioned the Zoom discussion in an earlier section). The Trust has many trustees and patrons who would be regarded as being affiliated with the

White supremacy of the British Empire and Monarchy. Halima condemned the report for denying the evil institutional racism yet has no problem accepting trustees and patrons affiliated with such a White supremacist and racist institution. These fine trustees and patrons are:

- Sir Clive Jones CBE (Chairman)
- Hossein Zahir QC
- Lord Parekh
- Baroness Amos
- Dame Diana Brittan CBE
- Lady Hollick
- Baroness Neuberger DBE
- Baroness Prashar CBE
- Baroness Whitaker

I have no problems with the honors system and various eminent titles. They are bestowed upon individuals who have made remarkable contributions to society. When given titles, this opens doors for them in the public arena and the corporate world because of their high standing. Their standing in society and subsequent utility would increase. Likewise, an organisation with such eminent people as part of its board would further enhance its reputation, thus attracting more investment or funding for its business or cause. Everyone is a winner. The aforementioned eminent people DESERVED their titles. I don't believe that they represent the old British White supremacy of colonialism and slavery because the Royal Family and Britain (including the Commonwealth of nations) are different today.

Question 23: (This is for the eminent CRED critics who have these honorary titles). Should you withdraw your titles to remain consistent with your views about current institutional racism's connection with British colonialism? If not, why not? For example, suppose you believe that the institution of the Monarchy no longer represents what it used to in the past. Why vehemently disagree with the CRED authors who convey a similar outlook?

Question 24: When the Duchess of Sussex, Meghan Markle, married into the Royal Family, why was she not condemned for marrying into a racist, White Supremacy institution?

Even though I firmly disagree with Afua Hirsch and Benjamin Zephaniah over political philosophies, I must give credit to them for their honesty and not falling into the trap of hypocrisy concerning the honors system and the British Empire. Professor Priyamvada Gopal of Cambridge University is fascinating. She is a Fellow of Churchill College. I visited Churchill College twice. Once after the 1997 General Election, when Conservatives faced a massive electoral meltdown, I was sponsored to attend a meeting of the 'Tory grandees' (veteran Conservatives) on restructuring the Conservative Party after its cataclysmic defeat. The second time was in 2018 when I attended a Parliamentary Assessment Board to re-enter the Parliamentary Candidates List (which would make one eligible to run for Parliament in a General Election). For me, it was a privilege to visit this college on both occasions. The college website states, "***Founded by***

Royal Charter in 1960, Churchill College is the national and Commonwealth memorial to Sir Winston Churchill, Britain's great wartime Prime Minister — the embodiment of his vision for how higher education can benefit society." Here is the problem. Priyamvada is affiliated with a college founded on a memorial to Churchill, whom she considers to be a racist. And given that the Commonwealth is a remnant of past colonialism, she is affiliated to a racist, commemorated by the Commonwealth, representing White supremacy colonialism.

Question 25: Should Professor Priyamvada Gopal continue to be affiliated with an institutionally racist college that commemorates a racist, reflecting the old British Empire via the Commonwealth? Discuss.

The Commonwealth of Nations

The British Empire no longer exists in its original form, but we have a Commonwealth of nations that were former territories of the British Empire. The English language and the common history of the Empire connect them. There are fifty-four member states, and the Queen is the Head of State for sixteen of them. If the Monarchy today is institutionally racist because of the genetic inheritance of past colonialism and slavery, then these fifty-four member states would have withdrawn their membership. These are free and independent states. Their governments and people are not stupid.

Given that they remain members shows that the Monarchy and Commonwealth today is seen in a different light compared to their past. These free and independent states have signed up to the 'Commonwealth Charter.' This charter upholds human rights, democracy, peace and security, equality, civil society, good governance, the rule of law, etc. Principle 4 is entitled, **Tolerance, Respect, and Understanding.** It states, *"We emphasize the need to promote tolerance, respect, understanding, moderation and religious freedom which are essential to the development of free and democratic societies and recall that respect for the dignity of all human beings is critical to promoting peace and prosperity. We accept that diversity and understanding the richness of our multiple identities are fundamental to the Commonwealth's principles and approach."*

Question 26: How does the Commonwealth Charter, especially Principle 4, uphold past slavery and colonialism?

Question 27: Should the fifty-four member states withdraw from the Commonwealth? Why or why not?

Should Past Vices Inform How To Treat Muslims?

Should the past vices of the Catholic Church or the Muslim empires inform how the Catholic Church or Muslims should be treated today?

CRED critics who use the British Empire's history of colonialism and slavery to inform how the Monarchy and British institutions should be interpreted today as vessels of institutional racism, are setting up Muslims and Christians for attacks.

The Catholic Church acknowledged regret and condemned their past where popes had called for the Crusades against Muslims to liberate the Holy Land. I enjoyed reading Pope John Paul II's book, *Crossing the Threshold of Hope.* Its message of peace and unity, especially with Muslim brethren, contrasts the Popes of the past who treated Muslims as the enemy. NO MUSLIM TODAY would hold into account Pope Francis or the Catholic Church for past atrocities. Some Muslim terrorists misuse the past Crusades to launch their crusade of terrorism against innocent people. But the two billion Muslims do not see the Catholic nor Protestant churches negatively because of past histories. This is the correct approach. Suppose the ghosts of the British Empire feeds into today's discourse on how we interpret racism. In that case, this view encourages our Muslim communities to view our Christian brethren negatively because of negative histories. We should not fall into this trap.

Likewise, Muslims of today are spiritual descendants of the past Islamic Empires. The Muslim civilisation had contributed to humanity through science, medicine, technology, and agriculture. This is accepted in Western academic discourse. However, there has been a negative side concerning the Ottoman Empire, where under its rule, one million Armenians were killed in a genocide between

1915 – 1917. President Joe Biden formally acknowledged this on April 24, 2021.

Question 28: Should Armenians consider Muslim countries today (especially Turkey, which is the descendant of the Ottoman Empire) as being institutionally racist against Armenians because of its genocidal history? The answer would be no. But the proponents of the idea of connecting today's Britain and the Monarchy to its past colonialism and slavery are doing precisely that. They are setting up the field for attacks against Muslims and Christians because of their negative past.

Question 29: Should Christians today view Muslims in the context of past histories of the Crusades? The Muslims/Moors were the enemies who captured the Holy Land and needed to be removed to liberate it. Should Christians today have a grudge against Muslims about past encounters with the Muslim empires?

Question 30: Should our Hindu cousins in India begrudge the one hundred twenty million Indian Muslims because of the historical legacy of the Muslim Mughal Empire that ruled India for over two hundred years?

The critics who link past British slavery and colonialism to today's institutions have not thought this through. They are setting up other communities for attack because of their past histories with Muslim and Christian empires. There are other empires that we could delve into and examine their effects today, but that is beyond the scope of this book. However, I have a burning question.

Question 31: For those critics who believe that capitalism is evil and that the past British Empire was 100% evil, what are your thoughts about the USSR (Union of Soviet Socialist Republics)? It may not have been technically an empire, but it had Eastern European countries under the Union with a centralized government and a centrally planned economy. Do you believe this system was better or worse compared to capitalist countries? Please marshal evidence to support your points.

Take Lessons from Bangladesh and Pakistan

Bangladesh celebrated its fifty years of independence on March 26, 2021. Halima Begum and I discussed this in public (separately) and what this meant for Bangladesh and its UK diaspora. Our parents have also told us what they witnessed first-hand.

The atrocities the Pakistan Army had carried out against freedom fighters were horrendous. All foreign dignitaries visiting Bangladesh are taken to the National Martyrs Memorial outside Dhaka to commemorate these freedom fighters' sacrifices. The Prime Minister of India, Narendra Modi, visited Dhaka in March 2021 to celebrate fifty years of independence. His presence was graciously received, more so because India had helped Bangladesh in its liberation. The Prime Minister of Pakistan, Imran Khan, was also invited to attend the ceremony. He would have attended had it not been for his COVID infection.

However, he sent a message of peace, harmony, and mutual co-operation. I believe that the Bangladeshi Prime Minister, Sheikh Hasina, was generous to invite Imran Khan. And for his message to be read out to the people of Bangladesh (amounting to around one hundred sixty-five million) is a new chapter in Bangladesh-Pakistan relations.

The Pakistan Army's atrocities inflicted on Bengalis in 1971 are never forgotten (it would serve Pakistan well to include this part of their history in their national curriculum). However, this does not determine how we interact with the new generation of Pakistanis today. Remember, this happened fifty years ago, so a generation alive today has lived through the oppression, and some of the freedom fighters are still alive today to recount their stories. But we refuse to construct our future by being shackled to the past atrocities inflicted upon our people. Bangladesh is free; it is empowered and on course to become a developed nation by 2050.

Back to the UK. When the CRED critics insist that institutional racism exists in Britain today because its history of colonialism and slavery is alive and well, they imply that the BAME communities are still shackled to the colonial past through institutional racism and do not have the power nor the capabilities to succeed unless the entire system is brought down. This is an insult to the BAME communities. While slavery and British colonialism have ended, the mindset where BAME communities are still shackled to the past and powerless to do anything is still alive and well -- a systemic mindset of disempowerment.

Why Are we Speaking and Writing in an Institutionally Racist Language?

If the above discourse has not convinced the CRED critics to re-evaluate their paradigm, consider this point. The English language is one of the gifts of our Empire. What was a language of the slave masters and colonialists is now an international language that enables trade and communications across borders. Thus, English is no longer seen as a medium of communication by slave masters. Instead, we have given it a new meaning.

However, if we utilize the logic of the critics of the CRED report and accept that the Monarchy and other institutions are systemically racist because of past colonialism and slavery, which merit dismantling, then what of the English language?

Question 32: Why do the critics still write and speak in the language of the slave masters?

Question 33: Why isn't there a concerted effort to seek an alternative international language like Esperanto?

Question 34: What purpose does it serve to continue speaking and writing in English (some of the CRED critics have an excellent mastery of the language of the slave masters)?

Migrants and Immigrants Are Not Stupid

Migrants who seek better lives for themselves and their families gravitate to countries that have better environments than their home countries. I am only referring to economic migrants and not refugees from war-torn countries (where Western countries have partly exacerbated conflict).

Question 35: Why would migrants travel to a country like the UK or USA, or Canada where institutional racism exists based on past slavery and colonialism and have poor outcomes unless these institutions have been pulled down (some academics mean the dismantling of Capitalism)? Why would economic migrants travel from a bad place to a worse one?

Question 36: Given that economic migrants generally migrate to the West, there are positive elements in their destination countries that merit such attraction. What are these positives for BAME migrants, and how do these positives exist under the umbrella of institutional racism?

The Acceptability of Racism – From Diversity and Inclusion to Divisiveness and Exclusion

The most painful episode of this sorry saga was the coordinated optimisation of racist rhetoric against the BAME commissioners of the CRED report. Nine out of the ten authors are from BAME backgrounds. What should have been a robust, polite, and civil debate between people with diverse opinions ended up in condemnation of the report without thorough examination. There was a flurry of racist abuses against these authors by the very people who believe institutional racism exists. Some examples of racist abuses against the authors are:

- The Chairman of the CRED report has been described as a Bounty bar (dark on the outside, White on the inside)

- They described The BAME commissioners as servants of their White master, Prime Minister Boris Johnson

- The Labour MP, Clive Lewis, tweeted a picture of a KKK clansman, with the caption, *'Move along nothing to see here.'*

- Professor Priyamvada Gopal of Cambridge University equated Tony Sewell With the Nazi general, Goebbels, because they both hold doctorates. On a lesser note, I read one of her tweets where she labeled Rakib Ehsan a 'chamcha.' Rakib was a researcher for the Henry Jackson Society until recently. He is now an independent analyst. He gave broad support for the CRED report, which is why he won this label. 'Chamcha' means ass-kisser in slang. This word is usually used in South Asia to describe a lackey of the

White man. I am not sure whether this word is racist; it depends on the meaning that is intended. But there should be an agreement that equating Tony Sewell with a Nazi is racism of the highest order.

These are not micro-aggressions. Neither are they macro-aggressions. These behaviors are off the scale, so I cannot put a label. Whatever it is, it is not ok. To advocate the ending of racial discrimination, only to hurl racist abuses at people who have divergent opinions, is a magnificent jump into the hyperspace of cognitive dissonance. These are the people who want to dismantle institutional racism. Work that one out. Tony Sewell is acting against Clive Lewis MP for his KKK tweet. I don't know if this will work. BAME racists need the same education that many White folks have had concerning unconscious bias and White privilege training. Because someone belongs to a BAME group does not give them the right to launch racist attacks on their adversaries who share the same BAME phenotype. This is the same type of unconscious bias training these racists need.

Another fascinating insight I garnered from this debate debacle is the bigotry or racism of groupthink. I mentioned this in my book, **United States of Anger**. That the Black or Brown colour of an individual should determine his politics is racism. When I joined the UK Conservative Party in 1995, I was told by many Asians that this was a mistake, that Labour was the party for Asians, etc. Fast forward to the 2020s, BAME politicians who belong to the

Conservative Party are dismissed by left-leaning journalists such as Afua Hirsch and Kehinde Andrews because they are in the wrong political party. Their black or brown skin colour should direct their affiliation to Labour or other Socialist groups.

I am a great believer in Diversity & Inclusion programmes rolled out in companies. I have consistently demonstrated that diversity is not just based on ethnicities but also opinions. If people cannot hold divergent opinions based on skin colour, then the phrase *'Diversity & Inclusion'* has no meaning.

Question 37: When we watch White folks argue and debate in the UK, they may support Conservatives, Labour, Liberal Democrats, the Green Party, and even Socialists/Communists/Marxists. In the US, they may support Republicans, Democrats, and other smaller parties. We expect to see an array of different opinions within these White groups; we do not expect them to hold one specific political philosophy because of their White skin colour. Yet, many on the left of politics would not afford this right to BAME groups if they wanted to hold divergent opinions. Why?

Question 38: What is it about Whiteness that makes it ok for them to have diverse opinions without being called a traitor to their race?

By now, the reader should amalgamate my arguments into a coherent understanding of the nuances of the debate, thereby formulating a disturbing conclusion. If the reader follows my train of thought, then our conclusions would resonate in harmony.

The critics of CRED who insist that institutional racism is set in stone, a remnant of vintage colonialism that subjugates BAME people today so that they cannot break through and succeed, are inadvertently propping up White supremacy. They are giving White supremacy the omnipotent and omniscient powers it does not have. They are relegating BAME people to a perpetual state of subjugation with no power nor freedom to break through glass ceilings. This is unconscious bias at its finest.

That is why I believe the CRED report is a relentless challenge to White supremacy rather than its impotent bedfellow. Little wonder why its authors have received a torrent of abuse and racial slurs and avoided discussing areas of commonality of which there are many.

Question 39: Could a systemic mindset be at play where White men are seen to occupy a superior (supreme?) status who are continuously oppressing BAME groups with no end in sight?

A similar scenario unfolded in the US after President Biden's speech to Congress on April 29, 2021. I watched the Republican senator, Tim Scott, respond to President Biden on behalf of the GOP. President Biden is still early in his presidency, so they should give him the support that any new President should expect from both sides of the aisle. Biden should continue to ensure that the vaccine roll-out continues at full steam ahead (at warp speed) in

America and developing countries. However, Tim Scott delivered an excellent speech, which I haven't heard for a long time.

Unfortunately, the racism of groupthink was in full swing from those on the progressive side of the aisle when they criticised him for holding 'wrong' views because he is Black. I am always amazed by Liberal/Progressives, especially White folks, who patronize Blacks/BAME by lecturing them on what racism is. For example, the White American broadcaster Joy Behar said that Tim Scott did not understand systemic racism because he said America was no longer a racist country. Unfortunately, Joy did not understand what Tim Scott meant. He was referring to systemic racism.

Twelfth Convergence

What is surprising is that Democrat Vice President Kamala Harris holds a similar view to Tim Scott. In response to Sen. Scott, Harris stated on ABC's *Good Morning America*, "***No. I don't think America is a racist country, but we also must speak the truth about the history of racism in our country and its existence today. I applaud the President for always having the ability and the courage, frankly, to speak the truth about it.***" Harris and Scott agree America is no longer a racist country (i.e., systemically, institutionally racist), and they agree racism still exists in society. This is what the CRED report states about the UK. I agree with Kamala Harris that the truth needs to be told about the history of racism in the US. The history of institutional racism in the U.S. is a history of the Democrat Party. This will be a good starting point.

Question 40: Why have Senator Tim Scott in the US and the CRED Commissioners in the UK been attacked (including racist insults) for claiming that institutional/systemic racism no longer exists in the U.S. and UK. However, they do not condemn Vice President Kamala Harris for holding a similar view?

Question 41: Our White liberal friend, Joy Behar, would seek to teach a Black senator about systemic racism. Would she also seek to teach the Jamaican Indian Vice President about systemic racism? If not, why not?

CNN's Van Jones did welcome Tim Scott's initiative to reform the police and reach across the aisle. But Jones said that if the Republicans had to produce someone like Tim Scott to respond to Biden, they must be in terrible shape. This is the bigotry of low expectations. Tim Scott's skin colour determined Van Jones's view that Scott must have represented the worst of the Republicans (the party of emancipation). BAME people need to think a certain way because of their skin colour, and if they don't, they must be an Oreo bar or a servant of White supremacy. It shows the racism of those who are fighting racism. A bizarre scenario that I have mentioned before.
(Stop press! After writing this section, I discovered the Chairman of the Lamar County (Texas) Democrat Party, Gary O'Connor, stated on a Facebook post, *"I had hoped that Scott might show some common sense, but it seems clear he is little more than an Oreo with no real principles."* Here we go again).

Interestingly, White folks have the privilege of holding diverse opinions, whether they are Labour, Democrats, Conservatives, Republicans, Green, Socialist, etc. No one would class them as traitors because they hold 'wrong' beliefs. Yet this privilege of diverse thinking is not afforded to BAME folks in the UK and the US. If they fall out of line and think differently (e.g., Conservative/Republican), they are traitors. This is an interesting insight into human psychology. Just as many White folks may not be aware of their privilege until someone points it out to them; in the same way, many on the Progressive/liberal side (especially White folks who like to lecture to Blacks) are not aware of their racist views, which needs to be pointed out too. Blacks are no longer on the plantation in the US, so their thoughts can no longer be controlled. Unfortunately, there is some residual 'plantation' mentality when they seek to point fingers at Black Conservatives for holding 'wrong' beliefs. Black Conservatives are at the receiving end of racist vitriol from many Progressives/Liberals, the same people who are at peace with their President who Kamala Harris once called out during the Democrat Primaries for supporting two racist segregationist senators,

... who believes that Black people are not Black if they vote Republican,

... and who has been accused of sexual harassment, where the victim was not believed.

Ah, but he is a Democrat, so that's okay.

My Criticism of the CRED Report and its Authors

The critics of CRED had microphones and megaphones, who received a lot of airtime as they condemned the report. The CRED authors do not need a megaphone but only a microphone because they have robust data to back them. I believe they should have been more challenging in engaging in debate with its critics. They would have done justice to BAME groups who have and continue to succeed in all areas of life. Unfortunately, the lived experiences of BAME successes are not taken seriously by the critics. They continue to push us down to the level of subjugation of our White colonial masters.

There is a marvellous irony. Many critics of the report agree with one of its recommendations. That is to dismantle the term 'BAME.' The reader will note that I have used this term one hundred forty-six times in this book unashamedly. I disagree with the CRED suggestion, but the critics agree on this. This is a wonderful insight into how divergent our synaptic connections are (i.e., between the critics and me). During D&I meetings, I have always stated that BAME is not a homogenous group. There are many different cultures, beliefs, and ethnicities within BAME; in the same way, there are diverse White cultures and ethnicities with the White umbrella label. Hence, I see no problem using the term 'BAME,' but if there is evidence to show that this term is harmful, I am happy to re-evaluate my paradigm and shift it accordingly.

Is Race Relations in the UK an Example for Europe and the World?

The CRED report claimed that the UK is an excellent example to other countries of what race relations should look like. The critics of CRED poured a lot of scorn on this claim because of their beliefs that institutional racism still exists; hence CRED authors could not possibly make this claim. I had to think about this. Sometimes, the UK is a good example when compared to Europe. In other cases, the normalisation of anti-Muslim rhetoric by the far-right may filter into mainstream thought within ten years if it isn't challenged. My forthcoming book, *Why the Far Right are Far Wrong,* will challenge this White supremacist rhetoric head-on.

When the critics of CRED immediately launched attacks on the idea of the UK being an example of good practice, my Muslim experience kicked in immediately, and I interpreted CRED's claim through these lenses. Unfortunately, over the last few years, European intolerance against Muslim immigrants and Islam has been increasing.

- Concerning Halal/Kosher meat, Sweden, Norway, Iceland, Denmark, and Slovenia had banned ritual slaughter, as per Islamic and Jewish laws.

- In 2009, Switzerland banned the construction of new minarets because they symbolized the encroachment of Islam.

- In April 2021, the French Senate wanted to ban the hijab for girls under eighteen. Senators also approved the amendment to the bill, which states, ***"prohibition in the public space of any conspicuous religious sign by minors and of any dress or clothing which would signify inferiority of women over men."***

- In 2016, A Muslim woman wearing a burkini lay on a beach in Nice (France) and was approached by four armed police officers, who told her to remove a part of her clothing. They published a photo of that incident in the media, and I noticed three women in their bikinis looking toward the Muslim woman. I thought to myself, *'where is that sisterhood to object to the armed police officers forcing a woman to remove her burkini?'* Some of the other beachgoers taunted the woman to go home—a fine example of bikini racism against burkinis.

- In 2018, Austria banned the 'niqab' or face covering.

These examples immediately kicked in when the critics of CRED condemned the report for stating that the UK was a beacon to Europe. I thought to myself that I am better off in the UK than in Europe. The critics should not have been so swift to condemn CRED's claim. However, there is a caveat to the above. The backlash against Muslims and Islam in Europe and the US is entirely the responsibility of Muslim extremists and terrorist renegades who misuse Islam for their death cult political ideologies. I have often stated in the media that our Muslim community must do more to drown out the extremists by not allowing them to abuse our religion. Little wonder why there is blowback through the rise of the Far-Right.

Whether the UK is a beacon to the world is more difficult to answer. It depends which countries are being compared. When I visited Malaysia in 2003, I was impressed with the racial harmony between the Malays, the Chinese, and the Indians. At that moment, I thought Malaysia was an excellent example to the world. I had always considered America to be a fine example of a nation of immigrants and how different ethnic groups lived in America and made progress over the last sixty years as proud Americans. Unfortunately, I am witnessing the divisiveness of Critical Race Theory (CRT) that seeks to divide ethnic groups, where debate is shutting down, thus giving way to intolerance. This a very bleak picture painted by Dr. Carol Swain, with whom I had a podcast with. The Judeo-Christian foundations of America as envisaged by its founding fathers are crumbling as we witness religious tradition being an object of mockery. I considered the most advanced nation on earth to be regressing as racial tensions break communities apart. I did not think this could ever happen. Hence, the UK is a good example to America of what race relations should be like, although it isn't perfect. The Conservative Government has not allowed CRT to permeate through academia, helping to slow down the slide toward racial intolerance. But the volcanic ashes of CRT from America are landing close to our shores. The United Nations body, SPUNHRC, stated in its criticism of the CRED report that it *"ignores the pervasive role that the social construction of race played in society."* Professor Priyamvada Gopal stated in her tweet, *"Race is a construct which has operational force. It is not unchangeable or biological."* (Tweet, 24th June 2020). CRT needs to be challenged head-on.

In religion, leaders in the UK pay lip service to religion to uphold secular values. However, the 400th anniversary of the *King James Bible* was celebrated in 2011, and it was refreshing to hear the Conservative ex-Prime Minister, David Cameron, mention the importance of Judeo-Christian religious tradition. I made a point on a BBC TV programme (*The Big Questions*) that Christians, Muslims, Hindus, etc., should uphold common religious traditions. This same cooperation should be seen in America, where religion is under attack. Interestingly, the CRED report mentions religion and culture as being factors that affect outcomes.

In relation to Muslim religious laws (Sharia), the country that serves as a beacon to Europe, UK, and America, is Israel. You heard me right. The intolerance of Islamic personal laws has percolated through European thought.

Still, unbeknown to Muslims, Israel is the only non-Muslim country which has Sharia courts that cater to Israeli Muslims (making up 20% of the Israeli population) and is on an equal footing with the Jewish Rabbinical courts, Christian courts, and secular courts.

Is the UK a beacon to Europe and the world? Sometimes, yes.

Weaknesses in My Arguments

Any objective person should expect to find weaknesses in one's arguments, however watertight they are. I am no exception. If the eminent critics respond to me and engage in constructive dialogue, and find holes in my arguments, I am more than happy to adjust my views. I don't have a big reputation to protect in front of the masses.

But if I run a self-diagnosis of my arguments, I can see one or two potential weaknesses. First, one of the CRED authors, Kunle Olulode, distanced himself from the report and condemned it for being selective of its presented data and lack of transparency. I don't know the ins and outs of this. Hence, I would welcome a discussion with him.

The other weakness is that I am not an academic. I am not a professor (although I have been nicknamed as one) nor a lecturer. I do not have the resources to conduct in-depth analyses, debates, and discourse with other academics whose fortes are race and colonialism. Instead, I write as a layman who asks questions. So, it should be easy for the critics, some of whom are professors or hold notable titles linked to the 'Most Excellent Order of the British Empire,' to provide robust counter-responses.

I look forward to that engagement.

The Star Trek Universe – A Message for my Fellow Trekkie, Patrick Vernon

Patrick Vernon wore his Star Trek uniform on a BBC programme to show that the CRED report came from another universe. I mentioned this earlier. However, in this section, I need to call out my fellow Trekkie buddy for something else. Patrick wore what appeared to be a blue t-shirt that represents a Starfleet officer, a doctor. Many inhabited planets in the fictional Star Trek universe belong to the United Federation of Planets, similar to the United Nations today. The respective symbols are similar. The alien species that are part of the Federation need to adhere to its rules and regulations. The Federation headquarters is based on Earth, and the high-ranking members within the Federation board are diverse, where different alien species are represented. Diversity and Inclusion at its finest. So far, so good.

But there is a group of renegades known as the Maquis who resist the Federation. Many species on other planets do not wish to be part of what they see as a colonial encroachment of their cultures. They refuse to join the Federation. Interestingly, the universal language, as translated by the universal translator, is American English.

So, the British-American Empire has reached the furthest corners of the universe through the United Federation of Planets. We are treated to a wonderful array of American English that the aliens speak. The blue Starfleet uniform Patrick wore to show disapproval of the CRED report symbolises galactic colonialism. He should have a problem with this even in this fictional universe. But then again, he might not. Given his title, '*Officer of the Most Excellent Order of the British Empire*,' I am sure he would make a good *Admiral* within Starfleet Command (the Federation's military, peacekeeping, and exploration wing). Unfortunately, my fellow Trekkie compatriot did not think this through.

BAME Breakthrough is Unstoppable – Message to the Youths

During Maajid Nawaz's show on LBC Radio, I gave some stark advice to the BAME youths. It is worth revisiting that audio link (p.4). The central part of the quote states, *"If there are glass ceilings, today you have the power, the tools, and the capabilities to break through these glass ceilings. Do NOT let anyone else dictate to you otherwise."*

Please cut out this quote and make sure your children put this up on their desks.

Question 42: I am taking part in a mentor programme where I will mentor a teenager from a BAME background. Should I inspire him or her with examples of successes and instil confidence for him to achieve some of his goals regardless of life's challenges, or should our conversation be about institutional racism and how he could not break through and achieve success until this is dismantled? Please furnish your answer with evidence.

Capitalists of the World Unite!

a) Why I Support the Marxist Co-Founder of Black Lives Matter

During my podcast with the eminent ex-professor, Dr. Carol Swain in America, I stated Conservatives should support the co-founder of Black Lives Matter, Patrisse Cullors. Patrisse had once declared she was a Marxist and reaffirmed this in December 2020 in her video response to her critics. Conservatives criticised her for spending over one million dollars to purchase a house in a leafy suburb of Los Angeles in a White neighborhood. No one in their right mind would move to an institutionally racist White supremacist neighbourhood. She has also bought other houses in nice neighbourhoods. There was general silence from supporters of Black Lives Matter, other than Hawk Newsome in New York, who stated that they should investigate BLM finances. I am not questioning Patrisse's finances. I assume they are from a legitimate source (she signed a deal with Warner Bros.).

Here is the reason Conservatives should support Patrisse and not call her out for her hypocrisy. Although she is Marxist in her thinking, her practical behavior was

Capitalist, even Conservative. That she reached a position where she could afford to buy houses in nice suburbs to secure her family's future and empower them is precisely what Conservatives and Capitalists advocate. Karl Marx had a problem with private capital and the institution of the nuclear family, as well as the greedy exploits of the bourgeoise. That Patrisse is having a paradigm shift toward the principles of Conservatism is a cause for celebration. This is her lived experience of success in the making. We should embrace her.

On a geopolitical level, the Chinese Communist Party took power in 1949 during their revolution in China. They confiscated land and abolished private enterprises. Soon afterward, there was widespread famine because of food shortages. In the 1970s, the Communist Party established a Capitalist framework. Since then, China has ushered in tremendous growth and prosperity for its people through globalisation, not colonisation, and is now a rising superpower. The economy is capitalist, but the government is Communist. Thus, China can be regarded as 'State Capitalism.' Likewise, India operated on a Socialist framework, following the Soviet-style of central planning. There was widespread poverty, but since the 1990s, when the finance minister Manmohan Singh (who would later become Prime Minister) opened India to the world economy, it is a rising superpower. Thanks to globalisation, inward investment, and focus on education and science, India achieved the tools and the power to become another rising superpower where poverty has declined. There is a rising middle class.

The lived experiences of success shown by Patrisse Cullors or the examples of phenomenal development of India and China ends all academic debates on whether Capitalism is inherently racist and geared against the poor. Capitalism is not anti-poor; it is anti-poverty.

These successes will not happen if White supremacist institutional racism or the effects of past colonialism are still at play. White Western colonialism would not have allowed the success of China's or India's rapid ascension to wealth and empowerment. Instead, both countries harnessed the tools of Capitalism (a facet of Conservatism) to empower themselves. No White supremacy organisation or institution can stop them. BAME success is here to stay and is unstoppable.

This mini discussion on world politics and Patrisse Cullors is relevant because these lived experiences of successes form the foundation of the CRED report, which focuses on the drivers for BAME empowerment and breakthrough. BAME communities do not have to wait for the collapse of institutional racism nor the dismantling of Capitalism (as many critics have argued) to be empowered for success. Instead, Capitalism is the powerhouse to extricate people from poverty by directing their trajectories toward prosperity.

This understanding became more poignant during the COVID-19 crisis. BAME people had been adversely affected because of higher comorbidities, catalysed by the crowded conditions many of them live in. The pandemic highlighted the economic disparities within BAME groups. This is even more reason Conservatives MUST work harder to implement policies to enable more BAME groups and even White working-class groups to escape the clutches of poverty toward prosperity. The ex-Prime Minister, David Cameron, coined the term, *'Compassionate Conservatism.'* I agree with this phrase, but more emphasis is needed on the 'passion' part. We know what works to empower people out of poverty into prosperity and where poor people become rich. These phrases would not feature in the vocabulary of those who wish to link Capitalism with racism, wishing its demise.

When Conservatives have done something for the poor, they have been met with scorn and ridicule. The *'Right-to-Buy'* scheme, which allowed tenants in social housing to buy the property they lived in, has helped many council tenants become homeowners, thus taking the first steps toward freedom and empowerment. Labour argued that this was unjust because privatisation of council houses reduced social housing available for those on the waiting list. The fact is that poor people had the opportunity to become rich through this scheme, which Socialists condemn. I came face to face with this Socialist thinking when I questioned the Socialist candidate, Lindsey German, for the London Mayor in 2004. I asked her how she would support those who wanted to better themselves.

She replied that they did not want to better themselves; they were quite happy where they were.

I recall how the Conservative Government under Prime Minister John Major helped low-income families in the 1990s by introducing the '*Assisted Places Scheme*' where bright children from low-income families could be eligible to receive vouchers to help pay for private education. A Bangladeshi friend told me how he benefited from the scheme when studying at a boarding school. He then went to a university and subsequently had a successful career working for the top consulting firms. He had the economic freedom to provide a nice home in a nice area for his family. His children's futures are secure. When the New Labour Government came to power in 1997 under Prime Minister Tony Blair, they abolished this scheme to my horror. Waging war on the poor by preventing them from succeeding is what Socialists do best. Socialism only works when poor people remain equally poor.

The health and economic disparities among BAME groups became more pronounced during the Covid pandemic. That is why there is an urgent need to reignite the passion for empowering the less fortunate and to go on the offensive.

Advocates for Socialism may send virtue smoke signals to bring down Capitalism by linking it with institutional racism only to benefit from Capitalism when they want to better themselves. Whether it is the Marxist, Patrisse Cullors, in the US who purchases nice houses in White areas to secure her family's future or some Labour MPs in the UK who send their children to the same schools that are advocated by Conservatives, or some critics of the CRED report who have attacked the commissioners and the institutional racism of the British establishment and monarchy, only to receive honorary titles at Her Majesty's pleasure. I agree with their decisions for themselves and their families; we must make sure these freedoms to make such choices for betterment and empowerment are extended to everyone else.

A side Note on Western multinationals

Those who seek to bring down Capitalism cite examples of 'greedy Western multinationals' exploiting third world countries. About twenty years ago, I attended a meeting in Parliament. The panel, chaired by the Labour MP Jeremy Corbyn (who would later become the Leader of the Labour Party), condemned Western multinationals and said they should return to their countries instead of exploiting developing nations. I posed a question to the panel. They forgot that there are Eastern multinationals that had expanded to the West. Does that mean they should return to their countries of origin? Or the Bangladesh multinational pharmaceutical company, Beximco, which expanded its operations in Western countries and Africa, India, and Asia, should it go back to Bangladesh? There was no answer. The correct answer is 'no.' This episode enlightened me about the bigotry/racism of low or no expectations. It did not occur to the panel that developing countries or Asian countries could also produce multinationals. Multinational corporations are not the remit of White nations only.

b) Is Capitalism Racist? A Response to the Labour MP, Zarah Sultana

Professor Kehinde Andrews mentioned the evil of Capitalism which promotes racism. The Labour MP, Zarah Sultana, stated a similar opinion on January 23, 2021, two months before the CRED report was released. She stated on Twitter, *"Racism in capitalist societies isn't a glitch. It's a feature. It's used to justify imperialism abroad and to divide and rule at home. That's why our anti-racism must be an internationalist socialism."*

The Soviet Union was internationalist in its Socialism/Communism. Section a) above stated how Capitalism has helped empower the poor locally, nationally, and internationally. In his work, *The Wealth of Nations*, Adam Smith stated, *"No society can surely be flourishing and happy, of which the far greater part of the members are poor and miserable."*

The debate on which political and economic ideologies transform the poor into rich, free, and empowered, has ended. The reason for drawing Capitalism, Socialism, and Marxism into this book about the CRED report and its critics is that I believe there is a looming ideological battle between Conservativism/Capitalism/religion and Socialism/Marxism/anti-religious tradition. This is the actual battle that is driving the debate around the CRED report. And BAME communities are tragically being used as pawns by one side through fear, anger generation, and permanent victimisation to control us. The nuclear attack on the CRED report is more easily explained now. If racism is declining, then there will be little need for anti-racism charities. These charities would be victims of their successes; thus, funding would decrease; they would be staring at their mortality. On a global scale, when capitalism empowers the poor and transforms previously developing countries into superpowers, then Socialism is staring at its mortality. When poor people become rich and free, there will be no more proletariat left to usher in a worldwide revolution against the greedy bourgeoise.

Zarah Sultana MP may be unaware of Karl Marx's essay on the Jewish Question. Marx stated,

> *"Let us consider the actual, worldly Jew – not the Sabbath Jew, as Bauer does, but the everyday Jew. Let us not look for the secret of the Jew in his religion but let us look for the secret of his religion in the real Jew. What is the secular basis of Judaism? Practical need, self-interest. What is the worldly religion of the Jew? Huckstering. What is his worldly God? Money. Money is the jealous god of Israel, in face of which no other god may exist. Money degrades all the gods of man – and turns them into commodities. The bill of exchange is the real god of the Jew. His god is only an illusory bill of exchange.... The chimerical nationality*

> *of the Jew is the nationality of the merchant, of the man of money in general... The Jew has emancipated himself in a Jewish manner, not only because he has acquired financial power but also because, through him and also apart from him, money has become a world power, and the practical Jewish spirit has become the practical spirit of the Christian nations. The Jews have emancipated themselves insofar as the Christians have become Jews...In the final analysis, the emancipation of the Jews is the emancipation of mankind from Judaism."*

This is what institutional racism looks like; in the case of Marx, racism against Jews (anti-Semitism) by linking their apparent greed for money with Capitalism. Just as there is encroaching Islamophobia by the Far Right seeping into mainstream thought today, I believe it won't be long before the Far Left adopts anti-Semitism as a by-product of their anti-Capitalist drive. The Labour Party under Jeremy Corbyn had their problems with anti-Semitism only recently. Still, I am uncertain whether Marx's Jewish question drove this or whether it was just a handful of rogue miscreants.

Question 43: Given that Marxism is an (institutional) ideology created by a White man who made racist statements against Jews, is Marxism/Socialism institutionally racist? Please elaborate on your answer.

Should the Government Withdraw the CRED Report?

Maybe, because it is not fit for 2021. However, it is ahead of its time by twenty or thirty years. Our Trekkie friend, Patrick Vernon, was not far off when he said that the report belonged to another universe. It belongs to another time in the future when everyone has accepted the fact that White supremacy and institutional racism are not omnipotent and that BAME groups have the power to succeed and break free from the shackles of the past. If the Conservative Government is in power, it MUST implement the twenty-four recommendations of the report and continue to be a relentless defender of the poor (including the White working-class) and BAME empowerment. No one else will lift them to the stratosphere of choice, freedom, success, and future security.

Having read my book, the reader should conclude that the CRED report recognises BAME achievements and provides twenty-four recommendations to close outstanding gaps. In my view, the CRED report is a direct challenge to White supremacy and a challenge to those who think that White supremacy and institutional racism are set in stone.

Question 44: Would the implementation of the twenty-four recommendations improve the state of BAME communities or make it worse? Discuss.

Conclusion – Message to the CRED Authors

The combined forces of attacks against the CRED authors through the medium of anger, rage, and copious amounts of virtue signalling should never have taken place. Vitriol and racist taunts have replaced robust debate against these authors. It was a painful scene to witness and peculiar indeed. Why did so many forces of anger and negativity combine so quickly to condemn the commissioners? That is why I aired my views on the radio on the day the report came out and subsequently followed up with this book. The flurry of activities in criticising the report reached a crescendo over a few days only to die down. This book will ensure that the debate is kept alive because I will not allow the vociferous critics of the CRED report to get away with their attacks.

I expect critics of the CRED report to respond in kind. They may not have been expecting a robust counter-response to their criticisms. But in the spirit of debate and dialogue, I hope we can continue the conversation for the sake of our communities. They can rest assured that I will incorporate their complete responses in this book for all to read, discuss, debate and benefit from.

As for the CRED authors, I do not know them personally. But I can feel what they had gone through when their reputations became recipients of nuclear-powered ad hominem attacks sprinkled with racism, sarcasm, and intolerance. It has been a bad time for them, the effects of which may remain for a long time. But they can hold their heads high because they are on the right side of history.

Replies from the Critics to my Invitation to Respond

At least two attempts were made to the following people to generate responses from them to the draft version of this book. In the interest of fairness, I invited them to ponder over my responses to their criticisms and then reply in kind, which would be captured in this book. Hence, I wanted to elevate this book from a mere polemic to a status of robust, constructive discourse and spirited debate. Here are the replies from the critics of the CRED report, whom I invited to retort.

Reply from David Lammy MP (Labour)

I received a note from the office of David Lammy MP. Unfortunately, he has a busy schedule, hence not available to engage in dialogue at this time. However, having worked with a couple of MPs, I know well how busy they are, so I respect David's commitment to his constituents.

Reply from Dr. Halima Begum (CEO of The Runnymede Trust)

Reply from Sir Simon Woolley CBE (Lord Woolley of Woodford)

Reply from Michael Hamilton

Reply from Professor David Olusoga (University of Manchester)

Reply from Professor Kehinde Andrews (Birmingham City University)

Reply from Professor Priyamvada Gopal (Fellow of Churchill College, Cambridge University)

Reply from Dr. Razai et al. (who published their letter to the British Medical Journal, 31st March 2021)

Reply from the Independent Experts of the Special Procedures of the United Nations Human Rights Council (who wrote a statement on 19th April 2021)

Hasan Imam

*Reply from Nadine Batchelor-Hunt (Political
Correspondent for Joe.co.uk)*

BAME: Breaking Through Barriers

Reply from Afua Hirsch (journalist and broadcaster)

Hasan Imam

Reply from Clive Lewis MP (Labour)

BAME: Breaking Through Barriers

Reply from Diane Abbott MP (Labour)

Hasan Imam

Reply from Bell Ribeiro-Addy MP (Labour)

Reply from Dawn Butler MP (Labour)

Hasan Imam

Reply from Zarah Sultana MP (Labour)

ABOUT THE AUTHOR

Hasan Ali Imam was born in Bangladesh and lives in the UK. He has been engaged in debate and dialogue over the last 30 years, culminating in his candidacy for the British Parliament in 2005. He continues to be involved with the UK Conservative Party in his spare time, while working full-time for a multinational corporation. Hasan has also been involved with the UK Government's 'Prevent' counter-terrorism strategy as a 'Trainer' to public servants on preventing young people from walking down the path toward radicalisation. Hasan believes in building bridges between divergent opinions and doesn't shy away from engaging in constructive debates. He regularly takes part in discussions on radio and TV in the UK and writes articles on various platforms.

Hasan Imam

Printed in Great Britain
by Amazon